Consolatory Rhetoric

Studies in Rhetoric/Communication
Thomas W. Benson, *Series Editor*

Consolatory Rhetoric

Grief, Symbol, and Ritual in the Greco-Roman Era

Donovan J. Ochs

University of South Carolina Press

The following publishers have granted permission to reprint specified passages from their copyrighted work: *Dio's Roman History*, trans. Earnest Cary (New York: G. P. Putnam's Sons, 1928); *The Illiad of Homer*, trans. Richard Lattimore (Chicago: The University of Chicago Press, 1951; Phoenix Books Edition, 1961); *Polybius: The Histories*, trans. W. R. Patton (New York: G. P. Putnam's Sons, 1927); Ronald L. Grimes, *Ritual Criticism: Case Studies in Its Practice, Essays on Its Theory* (Columbia: University of South Carolina Press, 1990).

Published in Columbia, South Carolina, by the
University of South Carolina Press

Manufactured in Canada

Library of Congress Cataloging-in-Publication Data

Ochs, Donovan J., 1938–
    Consolatory rhetoric : grief, symbol, and ritual in the Greco
-Roman era / Donovan J. Ochs.
        p.   cm. — (Studies in rhetoric/communication)
    Includes bibliographical references (p.   ) and index.
    ISBN 0–87249–885–9 (hard back : acid-free)
    1. Funeral rites and ceremonies—Greece—History.   2. Funeral
rites and ceremonies—Italy—Rome—History.   3. Funeral orations.
4. Rhetoric—Greece.   5. Rhetoric—Italy—Rome.   6. Greece—Social
life and customs.   7. Rome—Social life and customs.   I. Title.
II. Series.
GT3251.A2034   1993
393′.9—dc20   93–16393

"To Absent Companions"

Contents

Tables

Editor's Foreword

In this book Donovan J. Ochs explores the rhetoric of Greek and Roman funeral rituals. Ochs argues that to understand the discourse of Greek and Roman funerals it is important to regard the accompanying rituals not merely as part of the context of the discourse but as themselves rhetorical. Rhetoric, for Ochs, encompasses the whole realm of symbolic human action, and always raises the question of "*what* is being communicated to *whom*, *by what means*, and for *what purposes*." But, argues Ochs, whereas the ideal of discourse is univocality, ritual enacts a rhetoric that is multivocal, ambiguous, and evocative, and when discourse and ritual are interactive, as in a funeral, a complex of meanings arises that would not be possible for either to achieve separately.

The fundamental form of Greek and Roman funeral rhetoric, according to Ochs, is opposition—starting with the opposition of discourse to behavior and extending symbolically throughout the funeral to grief and consolation, separation and continuity, body and spirit. Read in this way, even the cemetery is a sign of the contraries of separation and continuity. Once the oppositional form is understood as fundamental to mourning rituals, writes Ochs, the interpretive frame and the rhetorical nature of the ritual are revealed. The oppositional form enacts the necessity of the mourners to make a choice between opposites—to choose life over death, renewal over endless and debilitating grief. In encouraging the choice of life and renewal, Greek and Roman funeral practices act as a rhetoric—a rhetoric for which Ochs offers a series of interpretations as they might have been situated in their own time and place.

Ochs argues that the ritual elements of funeral practices need to be understood as essentially communicative actions, and that funeral discourses need to be evaluated and understood from the perspective of rhetorical rather than literary standards. Hence, the stability of the rhetorical topics addressed in funeral orations is not a literary fault but a rhetorical achievement.

Funeral practices, writes Ochs, begin with the utter constraint of the fact of death, which no human word or wish can reverse. The forms that humans developed to ritualize burial were in their own turn highly constrained by persistent forms designed to provide the living with the means to structure their grief and console one another. The silent isolation of death is persistently answered by the affirmation of community.

Thomas W. Benson

Preface

No one ever writes a book without the help and support of many others. This effort is no exception; in fact, without the assistance and encouragement of my colleagues and students, this book would remain unwritten. My debts are extensive and these few words of recognition can only go a short distance to express my gratitude.

Consolatory Rhetoric had its beginning with a telephone call from Dierdre Johnston, a former graduate student and currently a faculty member at Carroll College, Waukesha, Wisconsin. She asked if I would agree to write and present a paper on Greco-Roman consolatory public address. Having taught units on the Greek funeral orations and Roman consolatory literature in my graduate courses for the past thirty years, I assumed, mistakenly, that her request would be easily fulfilled. I accepted the invitation and set to work. My research efforts very quickly convinced me that more, much more, was contained in Greco-Roman funeral rituals than close, interpretive readings of the funeral orations. The paper itself, hardly more than a preliminary sketch of the book's outline, was presented to the Health Communication Commission, a subsidiary of the Speech Communication Association. The response, advice, encouragement, and counterargument from the scholars in the audience, many unknown to me, provided motivation to give the project priority status.

A sequence of happy events rapidly followed.

The University of Iowa granted me a sabbatical in the spring of 1991 to work on *Consolatory Rhetoric*.

Two research assistants, Diana Liddle and Lee Artz, overwhelmed me with their enthusiasm, energy, and bibliographic expertise. Often, anticipating a request before I had time to make it, they secured references, photocopied material, and

xiii

ever so politely insisted that I move more quickly on the project. Diana and Lee deserve special recognition.

Preliminary drafts of my paper, distributed to my faculty colleagues—Professors Antczak, Trank, Cintron, and Biesecker of the Rhetoric Department and Professor Gronbeck of the Communication Studies Department—were returned with generous comments, corrections, and suggestions.

In the fall of 1991 I was most fortunate to be named an Iowa Faculty Fellow in the Scholars Workshop on Legal-Rhetorical and Philosophical Culture in Antiquity. This workshop, sponsored by the National Endowment for the Humanities and The Project on the Rhetoric of Inquiry (POROI), enabled me to see the work through to completion. Here, too, assistance and support were abundant. The co-directors of the workshop, Don McCloskey (Economics and History) and John Finamore (Classics), were generous with their encouragement and suggestions. I received valuable criticism on parts of the manuscript from my workshop fellows, John Kirby (Classics), Takis Poulakos (Classical Rhetoric), Janet Davis (Rhetoric and Classical Languages), and Trude Champ (director of the Iowa Translation Workshop). During my stay at the workshop I received every kindness and great administrative support from the workshop staff: Katy Neckerman (executive director of POROI), Judy Terry, and Jessica Drollinger. As revisions of the manuscript continued, James J. Murphy and Richard Enos, both longtime colleagues in the profession, offered excellent and detailed commentary. Then, near the end of the project, James McDaniel provided much needed assistance with the bibliography and index.

Three incredibly competent and cherished co-workers in the Rhetoric Department main office—Bonnie Bender, Cindi Stevens, and Deb Loss—must be recognized as key personnel in the production of *Consolatory Rhetoric*. Whether transcribing dictation, collating photocopy, typing manuscript, or scheduling appointments, their cheerful manner and flawless work never failed to make writing this book an enjoyable undertaking.

Whatever of value a reader may discover in this book must be shared among all who helped. Errors and shortcomings are mine. To each of you who took part in this project, please know that I am grateful.

Chapter One

Rhetoric and Consolatory Ritual

At some point in time all humans die. Each person's death has both impact and consequences, to a lesser or greater degree, depending on who the person was and the circumstances surrounding the death. After a death someone or some group of individuals conduct and participate in a funeral ritual. These rituals, ancient in origin and specific to a culture, are ceremonies designed to produce effects in the participants. Viewing funeral rituals from this perspective, I offer the single proposition around which this book is organized and toward which subsequent chapters offer support. Succinctly phrased, I argue that *in a funeral ritual, sets of symbols are placed in opposition to function rhetorically on the participants.* What, then, do the key terms in this proposition mean?

Rhetoric Defined

Historically, "rhetoric" has been generally associated with the activity of someone using language, spoken and written, to persuade. That is, after gauging an audiences' beliefs, attitudes, and values, a rhetor marshals materials, reasons, appeals, and claims into linguistic structures to effect change in an audience.[1] Lincoln's *Second Inaugural* and a used-car salesperson's pitch are equally included in the historical understanding of "rhetoric." From Aristotle's definition of rhetoric as "the faculty of discovering in any given case the available means of persuasion"[2] to Donald Bryant's specification of rhetoric as the act of a rhetor "adjusting ideas to people and people to ideas,"[3] the overriding emphasis is on verbal means and verbal persuasion of an audience by a speaker or writer. Admittedly, voice, gesture, and movement have also been part of the rubric of rhetoric since Classical times, but the predominant concerns have remained verbal, propositional, enthymematic,

1

and discursive. To use language rhetorically, then, is to use language to persuade.

Can other forms of human communication have suasory effects? Common observation indicates that such is the case. Songs and narratives can; burning crosses and spray-painted swastikas can; a child's gift of a handful of dandelions to his or her mother certainly can. Acting in an emotional state when it is reasonable to be in such a state is as rational as acting on the basis of demonstrable fact.[4]

For the present study I will define rhetoric as "the rationale of instrumental, symbolic behavior,"[5] a definition Professor John Bowers and I advanced some years ago. Lest a reader erroneously assumes this to be an unusual definition one needs, perhaps, to recall the recommendation of the rhetorical scholars attending the prestigious Wingspread Conference in 1970: "Rhetorical criticism must broaden its scope to examine the full range of rhetorical transactions; that is, informal conversations, *group settings*, public settings, mass media messages, picketing, sloganeering, *chanting*, singing, *marching*, *gesturing*, *ritual*, institutional and *cultural symbols*, cross cultural transaction, and so forth" (emphasis mine).[6]

To study funeral rituals, then, requires a conception of rhetoric broader and more inclusive than the traditional rhetor-oration-audience model of persuasion. One needs, rather, to adopt Wayne Booth's perspective that "rhetoric will for now be all the arts of changing men's minds"[7] or Kenneth Burke's view that symbolic action is persuasion.[8] George Kennedy, for example, defines rhetoric as "the energy inherent in communication."[9] He, too, believes that rhetoric in its broadest sense is "present also in physical actions, facial expressions, gestures, and signs generally,"[10] and that rhetoric "itself is a form of energy driven by a basic instinct to survive."[11]

At issue here is not the choice of either "traditional/verbal" or "new/symbolic" starting definitions. Particularly because funeral rituals contain and use verbal symbols (orations, sermons, eulogies, etc.) as well as a host of other types of symbols (processions, sounds, gestures, colors, dress, etc.), the wise choice is a "both . . . and" position. Accordingly, the symbolic behaviors used in funeral ceremonies within this study will include both the verbal and the other-than-verbal. In the funeral ritual both systems, each with its special strengths and limitations, are used to bring about culturally intended effects. As such, the suasory nature of this dual system can be properly construed as rhetorical and an appropriate subject area for rhetoric analysis.

Often, the concept of a "rationale" in any definition of rhetoric becomes obscure or problematic for a reader. Here, the term is taken in its usual and customary signification. A rationale is an explanation and exposition of the principles, the rational foundation, of the instrumental symbolic behavior that comprises a funeral ritual. For example, one such principle might be stated, "To denote the separation function in the funeral ritual, it is necessary to clothe the body of the deceased in such a way as to reduce the ugliness of death for the participants." One task of the subsequent chapters in this book, therefore, is that of isolating and explaining the rational foundations, the principles, of symbolic behaviors in funeral rituals.

Symbol

In both the announced thesis of this book and in the definition of rhetoric previously advanced, three remaining terms require clarification—ritual, symbol, and opposition. We begin with symbol.

Etymologically a symbol is a sign by which one knows or infers a thing. *Webster's New International Dictionary* offers this denotation: "That which stands for or suggests something else by reason of relationship, association, convention, or accidental but not intentional resemblance; esp., a visible sign of something invisible, as an idea, a quality or totality such as a state or a church; an emblem; as the lion is the *symbol* of courage. The cross is the *symbol* of Christianity."[12] In our culture symbols abound. The American flag is the symbol of our country. A gold Patek Philippe wrist watch is a symbol of wealth. A gold band worn on the third finger of the left hand is, almost always, a symbol that the person is married. In other words a symbol is an intermediary, something located between what the symbol stands for and what someone confronts, understands, knows, or responds to. Clifford Geertz states this "location between" characteristic by noting that "a symbol is any object, act, event, quality, or relation which serves as a vehicle for a conception."[13] This conception is the meaning, for an individual, of the symbol.

One must sort out the different kinds of symbols, however, lest one assume that all symbols and symbol systems are identical. At the most important level of distinction, important for the purposes of the ensuing analysis of funeral symbols, is the division of symbols into verbal and other-than-verbal. Words are symbols which fit neatly into the several definitions thus far set forth. Our everyday talk is comprised of symbols, words that reflect the way we see our environment and words that define the items in it. Our words create things out there for us.[14] Words denote and connote. Words, once meanings are established, can be combined into grammars and logics to enable word-users to communicate and partially understand each other's ideas, needs, feelings, etc. Jurgen Ruesch and Weldon Kees, for example, extend the notion of what words can do in this way:

> In its denotative capacity a single word can refer to a general or universal aspects of a thing or event only. In order to particularize and specify, words must be combined with other words in serial order. Words enable us to express abstractions, to communicate interpolations and extrapolations, and they make possible the telescoping of far flung aspects of events and diversified ideas into comprehensible terms. . . . Verbal codifications are essentially emergent, discontinuous, and arbitrary.[15]

Our everyday life is also filled with other-than-verbal symbols. The term, "nonverbal communication," behaviors that accompany verbal communication, includes such forms as tone of voice, rate of speech, relaxation of posture, spatial distance, etc.

Symbols can also be codified into action language and object language. Action language "embraces all movements that are not used exclusively as signals," whereas object language "comprises all intentional and nonintentional display of material things."[16] Teaching someone how to properly tighten a bolt cannot be done with only verbal symbols; action and object languages must be used. Or, to offer a more complex illustration, an individual protesting a war might well march (action language) to a federal building (in object language a symbol of the government) while carrying a placard on which a verbal slogan is written in the individual's own blood (object language). Such symbolic languages are frequently used in contexts of social challenge and social disruption. Both individuals and groups encounter situations in which words are not enough, and additional registers of expression and meaning must be used. Action and object languages provide these registers. The death of individuals that cause or have the potential for causing major social upheaval, for example, call forth massive use of symbolic languages, e.g., President John F. Kennedy's funeral.

To sum up this discussion of symbols and symbolic behavior a comparative explanation might help. "We find it useful to imagine a continuum of symbolic behavior. On one end are words and other kinds of arbitrarily symbolic behavior, behavior for which no natural connection exists with what the behavior stands for, the referent. On the other end of the continuum is more naturally symbolic behavior, behavior in which the observer need go through no arbitrary set of rules to establish the relationship between the sign and between the sign and its referent."[17]

Ritual

The term ritual requires some clarification. As a time-honored object of study for anthropologists and sociologists and, more recently, political scientists, the term itself has yet to acquire a standardized, widely accepted definition. In our ordinary language, "ritual" is often substituted for "routine." Certainly, one's customary dressing behavior, e.g., left sock, right sock, left shoe, right shoe, can seem ritualistic in that the activity is repeated and the steps in the behavior are identifiable. Such behavior, however, is better classified as a habit or a routine since it lacks any important meaning for the individual. Nor, for that matter, does the behavior alter or change any significant beliefs the individual as a member of a group or community might hold.

If ritual is not routine what, then, might it be? Predictably, the experts disagree. Raymond Firth believes a behavior can be considered a ritual if "it follows *patterned routines*; is a system of *signs* that convey other than overt messages; is *sanctioned* by strong expressions of moral approval; and has *adaptive value* in facilitating social relations."[18] Esther Goody sees ritual as "that aspect of customary behavior that makes statements about the hierarchial relations between people."[19] Christopher Crocker stipulates that ritual "is a statement in metaphoric terms about the paradoxes of human existence."[20] Margaret Mead reduces the concept to "patterns of human behavior."[21] Edward Fischer offers the didactic claim that "all ritual is communication, as communication, ritual speaks to our minds, and spirits, and intuitions by means of words, sights, sounds, and smells."[22]

Rather than bemoan and summarily dismiss these definitional efforts, I believe it more prudent to consider Edmund Leach's cautionary explanation:

> Ritual is clearly not a fact of nature but a concept, and definitions of concepts should be operational; the merits of any particular formula will depend upon how the concept is being used. In short, to understand the word *ritual* we must take note of the user's background and prejudices. A clergyman would assume that all ritual necessarily takes place inside a church in accordance with formally established rules and rubrics; a psychiatrist may be referring to the private compulsions of individual patients; an anthropologist will probably mean "a category of standardized behavior (custom) in which the relationship between the means and the end is not 'intrinsic,' " but he will interpret this definition loosely or very precisely according to individual temperament.[23]

For one interested in the rhetoric of funeral rituals, however, the shortcoming in all of these definitions is the absence of concern about *what* is being communicated to *whom, by what means*, and for *what purposes*. Leach's observation could be construed as carte blanche in establishing the parameters of the term, ritual. Although the apparent offer is tempting, little understanding would result if the offer was accepted. Since the concept of the term clearly depends on who is using it, the user's purpose, and the context in which behaviors are labeled as ritual, one is better served by thinking of a ritual as a phenomenon possessing a group of qualities. Ronald Grimes in his book, *Ritual Criticism: Case Studies in Its Practice, Essays on Its Theory* contends that any single definition of ritual will prove incomplete if not actually counterproductive. Rituals have qualities, he argues, and "when these qualities begin to multiply, when an activity becomes dense with them, it becomes increasingly proper to speak of it as ritualized, if not a rite as such."[24] Grimes provides a table in which these qualities are displayed (Table 1.1).[25]

Far and away the best single encapsulation of the term appears in *Ritual, Politics, and Power* authored by David Kertzer. He defines ritual as "an action wrapped in a web of symbolism. Standardized, repetitive action lacking such symbolization is an example of habit or custom and not ritual. Symbolization gives the action much more important meaning. Through ritual, beliefs about the universe come to be acquired, reinforced, and eventually changed."[26] Kertzer also notes that "ritual helps give meaning to our world by linking the past to the present and the present to the future." Rituals also "provoke an emotional response." To the question of what is the content, the substance, and the important components of a ritual, Kertzer comes full circle and states, "Symbols provide the content of ritual."[27]

Symbolic Meaning in Ritual

To test whether something is acting as a symbol one can ask: does it condense meaning? Is it multivocal? Is it ambiguous?[28]

Symbols are richly diverse, that is, a panoply of actions and objects can serve as symbols. One need only reflect on the typical marriage ritual in our own culture to witness the use of such objects as candles, flowers, carpets, rings, veils, formal attire, etc. In the same ritual we see a number of actions used symbolically—a march, a "giving away," a joining of hands, a recessional, the throwing of rice, the decorating of the wedding car, etc.

Insofar as symbols are multivocal (in verbal systems univocality of terms is prized) a variety of different meanings can be attached. By way of illustration consider the multiple mean-

TABLE 1.1
QUALITIES OF RITUAL

- performed, embodied, enacted, gestural (not merely thought or said)
- formalized, elevated, stylized, differentiated (not ordinary, unadorned, or undifferentiated)
- repetitive, redundant, rhythmic (not singular or once-for-all)
- collective, institutionalized, consensual (not personal or private)
- patterned, invariant, standardized, stereotyped, ordered, rehearsed (not improvised, idiosyncratic or spontaneous)
- traditional, archaic, primordial (not invented or recent)
- valued highly or ultimately, deeply felt, sentiment-laden, meaningful, serious (not trivial or shallow)
- condensed, multi-layered (not obvious; requiring interpretation)
- symbolic, referential (not merely technological or primarily means-end oriented)
- perfected, idealized, pure, ideal (not conflictual or subject to criticism and failure)
- dramatic, ludic (i.e., playlike) (not primarily discursive or explanatory; not without special framing or boundaries)
- paradigmatic (not ineffectual in modeling either other rites or nonritualized action)
- mystical, transcendent, religious, cosmic (not secular or merely empirical)
- adaptive, functional (not obsessional, neurotic, dysfunctional)
- conscious, deliberate (not unconscious or preconscious)

ings an observer potentially could attach to the use of a "white carpet" at a wedding: they are rich; the parents are wasting money; just as the bride is "unsoiled" before the ceremony, the carpet ensures that she will remain so; or arrivals of important people are honored with carpets on which to walk and the bride is the center of the wedding and, justifiably, honored.

Ambiguity, a necessary property of symbols, relates quite closely to multivocality. Extending the "white carpet" illustration somewhat, one can begin to understand that each potential meaning may be true for the individual assigning a given meaning, but none can be considered correct or incorrect. Unlike verbal systems where general agreement about meanings is necessary for people to use the system to communicate, the ambiguity of *some* action and object symbols may have a considerable degree of general agreement. When the bride and groom kiss, for example, those participating in the ritual "need go through no arbitrary set of rules to establish the relationship between the sign and its referent." Yet, *some* action and object symbols may possess less general agreement as the "white carpet" illustration suggests. Since this is so, an important theoretical issues arises. Do the other-than-verbal symbols used in a ritual simply *evoke* meanings in participants, or do such symbols *refer* as do words in the verbal system?

Few, if any, would disagree that symbols used in rituals have evocative power. Most have witnessed the emotional outpourings of some persons who react at the appearance of the U.S. flag at a Veteran's Day parade. Referentiality, however, is another matter. The statement, "the salt shaker is on the table," is ordinary language with generally agreed upon meanings for the object and its location. No symbol in the language of actions or objects used in a ritual can possess this type of strict referentiality. However, verbal systems begin to lose referentiality as the terms used in the system move away from the sensible and demonstrable. For example, the statement "justice will prevail when equitability returns to the economic sphere" contains little, if any, sensible or demonstrable referent for the words used as verbal symbols. Language at this level of abstraction becomes both ambiguous and multivocal, properties of the other-than-verbal symbols used in rituals.

Another observation must be made. Participants in a ritual each bring a different degree of participation history to the event. A young child attending his or her first military funeral would conceivably be awestruck if not actually frightened by the unusual uniforms, close order drill commands, gun fire, and the playing of taps. Yet, the very unusual, special, and out-of-the-ordinary nature of this ritual, and all rituals for that matter, compel curiosity and inquiry. Across time and with repeated participation, the symbols in a ritual not only evoke emotional responses, feelings, and personal memories but increasingly refer to beliefs, attitudes, and values. Actions and objects used in rituals can be, and are, explained in words. Were one, for example, to ask the participants in a wedding ritual why the bride and groom exchange rings, multiple explanations would be forthcoming. Would all such explanations be identical? Not likely. Would the diversity of explanations be evidence to claim nonreferentiality for action and object? Not at all. While symbolic behaviors in a ritual cannot attain strict referentiality as can some verbal statements with sensible and demonstrable referents, these behaviors, when translated into verbal explanations can refer to abstract beliefs, social attitudes, and cultural values. As Leach argues, "culture communicates; the complex interconnectedness of cultural events itself conveys information to those who participate in those events."[29] He, too, argues that "individual items of observed behavior and individual details of custom can be treated as analogous to the words and sentences of a language."[30]

Opposition

A final term in the premise of this book requires clarification. The concept of opposition is used here in a simple relational sense. That is, two symbols are "in opposition" if they are set against each other, as different as possible from each other, contrastive, and each is the reverse of the other. The relationship itself is devoid of content since it is a form that can exist between terms and propositions as well as between positions, directions, movements, etc. The binary quality of this relationship did not go unrecognized or unused by the ancients.

Most human things go in pairs, for example, wet/dry or hot/cold. So fundamental is this observation that pre-Socratic scientists typically based their theories and explanations of phenomena on one or another kind of opposition. As Geoffrey Lloyd observes in his book, *Polarity and Analogy: Two Types of Argumentation in Greek Thought*, "Certain manifest natural oppositions, such as day and night, male and female, and perhaps especially right and left, are often taken as the symbols or embodiments of fundamental religious or spiritual antitheses (pure and unpure, blessed and cursed)."[31]

At a general level one can see displayed within the three phases of the funeral rite of passage the symbolic behaviors, verbal and other-than-verbal, and the elements of these behaviors. A number of these features, however, merit further development.

In other words, for the early Greeks, the presentation of linguistic opposites—contradictories, contraries, and subcontraries— "provide simple and distinct reference points to which other things may be related."[32] *One term is valued; the other is devalued.* This same principle holds for action and object languages as well. An hypothetical example will illustrate this point.

Assume that a person must decide which of two close order drill teams is the best. One group wears identical tailored uniforms, executes complex maneuvers in perfect synchrony, and completes their movements with apparent effortlessness. The other group wears mismatched and disheveled clothing, stumbles and falters during attempted group movements, and appears exhausted while doing so. The point should be clear: the presentation of juxtaposed oppositions functions persuasively by forcing a choice; and the direction of the choice is imbedded within the form itself as well as the cultural values attached to the items fixed in each side of the polarity. Symbolic behaviors can be and are placed in oppositional forms in the funeral rites of the Greco-Roman Era.

Symbolic behaviors are actions, something done for purposes other than mere movement or simple display. These actions involve doing or accomplishing some end. As symbols they condense meaning and retain the characteristics of ambiguity and multivocality. Like a word, a symbol is meaningless without syntax or a pragmatic context. In addition, symbolic behaviors do contain elements, defined as those parts of an action capable of being sensed, recognized, and responded to. Stated in other terms an element, in the sense used here, would be those sensory items someone from another community and another culture would use in describing a funeral ritual. For example, the Archaic Greek practice of each funeral attendee placing a lock of his or her own hair upon the remains of the deceased at the burial phase would be noted. Interpreting this element outside of the communal ritual of which it is a significant part would prove quite difficult for such an "outside" observer. Symbolic behaviors and their elements need to be interpreted in the context in which they occur. Grasping the interconnections of context, phases of the ritual, the opposing and reinforcing symbolic behaviors, and elements of a given behavior is a considerable undertaking.

Before proceeding further, then, the controlling thesis of this book can now be expanded in light of the discussions and definitions of key terms. In a funeral ritual, an action wrapped in a web of symbolism, sets of symbols and their elements—verbal, action, and object languages—are placed in opposition to function rhetorically, that is, through the rationale of instrumental symbolic behavior, on the participants.

Scope of the Study

One can raise the legitimate question, why write a book on consolatory rhetoric? Can such a perspective yield anything of importance not already observed by anthropological field studies, sociological treatises, and historical accounts of funeral rites and rituals? Might any useful insights be added to studies undertaken by rhetorical historians and critics who have analyzed and assessed Greek funeral oratory and Roman consolatory discourse? Each reader of this book, of course, will render his or her own answer to these questions, but something of a preliminary answer is in order.

Although it may seem quite obvious, scholars subscribe to and are conscripted within their academic specialty. That is, sociologists are primarily concerned with studying collective behavior. Funeral ceremonies, being a particular instance of collective behavior, provide excellent arenas for sociological description and commentary. In a similar manner, anthropologists study human beings, their environment, social relations, and culture. Neither the sociologist nor the anthropologist, nor, for that matter, the historian or classicist undertake the study of people using symbol systems to affect the belief, attitude, and value systems of an audience. Such is the province of the rhetorician working as a critic of symbol systems used for suasive ends. Nonetheless, the exceptional work of many scholars in these related disciplines provides the basis on which rest the detailed arguments of symbolic consolation in subsequent chapters. With their descriptions, evidence, and research, this book rests on a firm foundation.

Until recently, rhetorical critics, influenced by Lester Thonssen and A. Craig Baird's *Speech Criticism*,[33] focused their analytical energies on major speeches of prominent individuals or, if not spoken persuasion then most certainly written discourse penned by prominent individuals. Kenneth Burke's pentad (act, actor, scene, agent, agency) has the potential for broadening a critic's point of view to consider more than a speech or persuasive document. Scenic analysis, if done at all, tends to remain at an elemental, descriptive level. By examining consolatory rituals in the Greco-Roman Era in terms of symbolic behaviors addressed to relevant audiences, one can gain new understanding and insight about the human uses of symbols and symbolic behaviors in consolatory settings.

Rituals of consolation, filled as they are with symbols, used rhetorically, need to be viewed as attempts to persuade. The incredibly heterogeneous nature of those who attend and participate in funeral rituals require more than a eulogy can be expected, realistically, to provide in addressing their individual and collective emotional and cognitive concerns. Studying funeral rituals from the perspective of rhetoric can forcefully demonstrate, as no other discipline can, the human and humane uses to which symbolic behavior can be marshaled in order to cope with and exert control over the all-encompassing consequences of an individual's death.

Symbolic Behavior and Rhetoric

How do the symbolic behaviors used in ritual function rhetorically? What is the inherent mechanism empowering these culturally acted out dramas? Kertzer points to the form of a ritual as the answer: "Ritual can be seen as a form of rhetoric, the propagation of a message through a complex symbolic performance. Rhetoric follows certain culturally prescribed forms

whose built-in logic makes the course of the argument predict-
able at the same time that it lends credence to the thesis advanced."[34] The key term here is form, specifically, although
Kertzer does not use the modifier, *rhetorical* form. The concept
is as old as rhetoric itself. "Classical rhetoric," Burke says,
"stresses the element of explicit design in rhetorical enterprise."[35] The twenty-eight topics of the enthymeme in Aristotle's *Rhetorica* are forms into which verbal arguments can be
fitted. One of his forms consists of the conditional premise
mode from logic wedded to the rhetorical form of opposition: if
war is the cause of our present problems, then peace will be the
best solution.[36] The substance in the apodasis of the proposition
is anticipated in the protasis and, when the form of opposition
is presented, a resolution, a certain mental settling into itself,
happens.

Rhetorical theories from the Greco-Roman Era include
much discussion of "explicit design" or, in simpler terms, rhetorical forms. Usually located in the theorists' discussions of
style, rhetoricians recognized, used, and taught lengthy catalogs of forms that invited assent by sheer mental completion of
the form. Such catalogs would list, for example, climax, review,
digression and return, over and understatement, enumeration,
interrogation, etc. In each of these and other rhetorical forms,
an audience is invited to collaborate and, by collaborating, offer
acceptance. Burke makes the point well.

> At least we know that many purely formal patterns can
> readily awaken an attitude of collaborative expectancy in
> us. For instance, imagine a passage built about a set of
> oppositions ("*we* do *this*, but *they* on the other hand do
> *that*; *we* stay *here*, but *they* go *there*; *we* look *up*, but *they*
> look *down*," etc.). Once you grasp the trend of the form, it
> invites participation regardless of the subject matter. For-
> mally, you will find yourself swinging along with the suc-
> cession of antithesis, even though you may not agree with
> the proposition that is being presented in this form. . . .
> And, this attitude of assent may then be transferred to the
> matter which happens to be associated with the form.[37]

Quite obviously, the form of the symbolic behaviors used in funeral rituals adds much to the rhetorical effort. As a persuasive

undertaking such rituals depend, for the degree of success they attempt to bring about, on the form of opposition both in the verbal and other-than-verbal symbols. Subsequent chapters will explicate and demonstrate how this was the case with funeral rituals in the classical era.

Classical Focus

Restricting the scope of this book to the Greco-Roman Era is a deliberate decision. At no other point in history was the study and practice of verbal persuasion so closely intertwined. Rhetoric was the center and the culmination of the school curriculum; oratorical skill was prized. Those who theorized the nature, causes, types, and effects of persuasion did address— in varying degrees of thoroughness—the rationale of persuasion in situational contexts. One of these contexts was that of a funeral. What one should *say* in a funeral oration and the reasons for framing such oratory remain accessible for us. Subsequent chapters draw on this legacy of theoretical material.

In the Greco-Roman Era oratory was considered an art form and a number of funeral orations remain available for study. These, too, provide one with actual illustrations of the language used at certain points in the funeral rituals. Consequently, the relationship between the theory and practice of verbal persuasion at funerals is more easily studied than in other historic periods. These classical rhetoricians and funeral orators, however, offer no insight into the other-than-verbal symbols used in the ritual. For these descriptions an abundance of evidence remains in literary accounts, their works of history, and the considerable body of archaeological material, e.g., paintings and sculptures depicting actual funeral practices as well as inscriptions and burial practices. In other words the material and evidence for studying symbolic persuasion in the Greco-Roman Era is available, accessible, and unexamined.

Restricting this book to the classical practices of the Greeks and Romans allows the interested reader to gain an historic vantage point from which to begin appreciating, recognizing, and interacting with present day symbolic behaviors of consolation. Indeed, as later chapters will suggest, many of the symbolic languages used in Greco-Roman funeral rites continue to be used in Western societies. That such is the case ought not be surprising; Rome borrowed from Greece and Christianity borrowed much from Rome. Then, too, a group's response, reaction, and reconstruction after the death of one of its members seems to admit to a finite number of symbolic behaviors. For example, the order of the march for a Roman's funeral procession is quite similar to those we encounter in our own cities and towns. Eulogists, then as now, address the virtuous deeds of the deceased.

The arrangement of the subsequent chapters calls for a few prefatory observations. Chapter 2, Death and Its Effects, addresses the rhetorical situation created by a death for the survivor who, in turn, may be a sole survivor, a significant other, a family member, a friend or acquaintance, a community, or in some cases, a nation or group of nations. To determine what the effects of death are, I have relied on the now considerable body of literature and research on death, grief, mourning, and bereavement as well as the literature on death customs and funeral practices.

A potential danger immediately arises. The tendency and impulse to project, to read the past in terms of the present must always be done cautiously, if done at all. Indeed, today's funeral ceremonies are apparently different from those of Greece and Rome. However, this book hinges on an assumption, namely, *the phases of personal bereavement are universals independent of culture*. There is no reason to doubt that the shock, sense of loss, grief, and pain experienced by the parents who lost a son or daughter in Vietnam or Iraq is different in degree or kind from those experienced by parents who lost a son in the Persian or Peloponnesian or Punic Wars. Admittedly, and this is an important distinction, cultural norms differ. Weeping in public, for many of us, is viewed with disapproval; the Greeks and Romans had different norms. Chapter 2, therefore, develops the components of the consolatory situation, a situation that rhetorical, symbolic behaviors need to address. Chapters 3 and 4 analyze the funeral rites of the Greeks; chapters 5 and 6, the Romans.

This book is written, primarily, for students of classical rhetoric. In some small way this book may highlight the significant contributions—and shortcomings—of the classical treatises on persuasion and their relationship to the people who lived—and died—in the Greco-Roman culture. I will assume that most readers of this book possess little, if any, facility with the classical languages and, therefore, I will make every effort to avoid unnecessary technicalities of translation. Others, too, may find something of value in the following chapters. If, indeed, one's realization of the role of symbolic behavior in consolatory situations is heightened and expanded, this book will have fulfilled one of its objectives.

NOTES

1. See also for representative scholarship: Lester Thonssen, *Selected Readings in Rhetoric and Public Speaking* (New York: The H. W. Wilson Co., 1942); John Quincey Adams, *Lectures on Rhetoric and Oratory*, ed. J. Jeffrey Auer and Jerald L. Banninga (New York: Russell and Russell, 1962); Marie Hochmuth Nichols, *Rhetoric and Criticism* (Baton Rouge: Louisiana State University Press, 1963); Dudley Bailey, *Essays on Rhetoric* (New York: Oxford University Press, 1965); Chaim Perelman and L. Olbrechts-Tyteca, *The New Rhetoric: A Treatise on Argumentation*, trans. John Wilkinson and Purcell Weaver (Notre Dame, IN: University of Notre Dame Press, 1969); Walter R. Fisher, *Rhetoric: A Tradition in Transition: Studies in Honor of Donald C. Bryant* (East Lansing, MI: Michigan State University Press, 1974); Richard Peter McKeon, *Rhetoric: Essays in Invention and Discovery* (Woodbridge, CT: Ox Bow Press, 1987); Brian Vickers, *In Defense of Rhetoric* (New York: Oxford University Press, 1988); George Kennedy, *Aristotle On Rhetoric: A Theory of Civic Discourse* (New York: Oxford University Press, 1991).
2. Aristotle, *Rhetorica*, 1.2.2.
3. Donald C. Bryant, "Rhetoric: Its Function and Scope," *The Quarterly Journal of Speech* 39 (December, 1953):418.
4. Wayne C. Booth, "The Scope of Rhetoric Today: A Polemical Excursion," in *The Prospect of Rhetoric: Report of the National Development Project*, eds. Lloyd F. Bitzer and Edwin Black, 93–114 (Englewood Cliffs, NJ: Prentice-Hall, Inc., 1971).
5. John Waite Bowers and Donovan J. Ochs, *The Rhetoric of Agitation and Control* (Reading, MA: Addison-Wesley Publishing Company, Inc., 1971), 2.
6. *The Prospect of Rhetoric*, 225. Italics, my own.
7. *The Prospect of Rhetoric*, 95.

8. Kenneth Burke, *Language as Symbolic Action: Essays on Life, Literature, and Method* (Berkeley, CA: The University of California Press, 1966). Also Sonja K. Foss, Karen A. Foss, and Robert Trapp, *Contemporary Perspectives on Rhetoric* (Prospect Heights, IL: Waveland Press, Inc., 1985), ch. 7.

9. George A. Kennedy, "A Hoot in the Dark: The Evolution of General Rhetoric," *Philosophy and Rhetoric* 25 (1992):2.

10. Kennedy, "A Hoot in the Dark," 4.

11. Kennedy, "A Hoot in the Dark," 20.

12. *Webster's New International Dictionary of the English Language*, 2d ed., ed. William Allen Neilson (Springfield, MA: G&C Merriam Co., Publishers, 1939), 2555.

13. Clifford Geertz, "Religion as a Cultural System," in *Anthropological Approaches to the Study of Religion*, ed. Michael Banton (London: Tavistock, 1966), 5. See also S. R. F. Price, *Rituals and Power: The Roman Imperial Cult in Asia Minor* (New York: Cambridge University Press, 1984). Price notes that, "The suggestiveness of symbols . . . offers a crucial way for people to handle types of knowledge which do not fit into either the semantic or encyclopedic categories." (9). Also Mary Douglas, *Natural Symbols: Explorations in Cosmology* (New York: Random House, 1970) and her subsequent work in *Implicit Meanings: Essays in Anthropology* (London: Routledge and Kegan Paul, 1975).

14. Peter Berger and Thomas Luckman, *The Social Construction of Reality* (New York: Doubleday and Co., 1966).

15. Jurgen Ruesch and Weldon Kees, *Nonverbal Communication: Notes on the Visual Perception of Human Relations* (Berkeley, CA: The University of California Press, 1959), 193. See also Alfred G. Smith, *Communication and Culture: Readings in the Codes of Human Interaction* (New York: Holt, Rinehart and Winston, 1966); Richard Hoggart, *On Culture and Communication* (New York: Oxford University Press, 1972); Paul Newell Campbell, *Rhetoric — Ritual: A Study of the Communicative and Aesthetic Dimensions of Language* (Belmont, CA: Dickenson Publishing Co., 1972); and Richard Hoggart, *Perspectives On Silence*, ed. Deborah Tannen and Muriel Saville-Troike (Norwood, NJ: Ablex Publishing Co., 1985).

16. Ruesch and Kees, *Nonverbal Communication*, 189.

17. Bowers and Ochs, *The Rhetoric of Agitation*, 2–3.

18. Raymond Firth, "Verbal and Bodily Rituals of Greeting and Parting," in *The Interpretation of Ritual: Essays in Honour of A.I. Richards*, ed. J. S. La Fontaine, 29–30 (London: Tavistock, 1972).

19. Esther Goody, "Greeting, Begging, and the Presentation of Respect," in *The Interpretation of Ritual*, 39.

20. Christopher Crocker, "Ritual and the Development of Social Structure: Liminality and Inversion," in *The Roots of Ritual*, ed. James D. Shaughnessy, 47 (Grand Rapids, MI: William B. Eerdmans Publishing Co., 1973).
21. Margaret Mead, "Ritual and Social Crisis," in *The Roots of Ritual*, 87.
22. Edward Fischer, "Ritual as Communication," in *The Roots of Ritual*, 161.
23. Edmund R. Leach, "Ritual," in *The International Encyclopedia of the Social Sciences*, ed. David L. Sills, vol. 13, 521 (New York: The MacMillan Co., 1968).
24. Ronald L. Grimes, *Ritual Criticism: Case Studies in Its Practice, Essays on Its Theory* (Columbia, SC: University of South Carolina Press, 1990), 14.
25. Grimes, *Ritual Criticism*, 14.
26. David I. Kertzer, *Ritual, Politics, and Power* (New Haven, CT: Yale University Press, 1988), 9. Those who wish to pursue the study of ritual can only profit from Grimes, *Research in Ritual Studies: A Programmatic Essay and Bibliography* (London: The Scarecrow Press, Inc., 1985). See also Sally F. Moore and Barbara G. Myerhoff, eds., *Secular Ritual* (Assen, The Netherlands: Van Gorcum & Co., 1977).
27. Kertzer, *Ritual, Politics, and Power*, 9–10.
28. Kertzer, *Ritual, Politics, and Power*, 11.
29. Edmund Leach, *Culture and Communication: The Logic By Which Symbols Are Connected: An Introduction to the Use of Structuralist Analysis in Social Anthropology* (New York: Cambridge University Press, 1976), 2. In this book Leach details the use of space and time in rituals (35), the indices of nonverbal communication systems (49), and such examples of binary coding as clothing (55), color (57), and silence (62).
30. Leach, *Culture*, 6.
31. Geoffrey E. R. Lloyd, *Polarity and Analogy: Two Types of Argumentation in Greek Thought* (Cambridge: Cambridge University Press, 1966), 38.
32. Lloyd, *Polarity*, 65.
33. Lester Thonssen and A. Craig Baird, *Speech Criticism* (New York: The Ronald Press Co., 1948).
34. Kertzer, *Ritual, Politics, and Power*, 181.
35. Kenneth Burke, *A Rhetoric of Motives* (New York: The World Publishing Co., 1962), 559.
36. *Rhetorica*, 2.23.1.
37. Burke, *Language*, 582.

Chapter Two

Death and Its Effects

Rhetorical Situations

Rhetorical discourse, the suasive use of symbols, does not simply happen at random. Something must happen or take place or be anticipated that unbalances the homeostasis of the situation in which one lives one's life. In his often cited essay, "The Rhetorical Situation," Lloyd Bitzer terms this "unbalancing" an "exigence."[1] When a state of affairs, marked by urgency, calls for or requires action, real or symbolic, the need for a rhetorical response is created. For example, were a group of urban land developers seeking authorization to buy a tract of woodland, quite likely a group of conservationists would develop arguments and, depending on the perceived degree of threat or loss, stage demonstrations to preserve the woodland. An exigence, for our hypothetical conservationists, brings forth the need for rhetorical acts. Similarly, a person's death causes an exigence creating a need for rhetorical action within a funeral ritual.

Suasive efforts by definition must be addressed, that is, directed at an audience and preferably at an audience with the power to resolve the exigence. Obviously, the dead person cannot be returned to life; the exigence here resides in those directly affected by the death. Their multiple needs are the ones that must be addressed. Audiences, Bitzer's second component of a rhetorical situation, may be more or less affected by a given exigence as well as more or less capable of effecting a desired change. A host of variables enter the audience matrix: material resources, duration of commitment, level of motivation, intensity and salience of competing suasive messages, etc. Still, for a rhetorical act to be recognized as such, an audience must be the recipient of the symbolic messages.

A third element, according to Bitzer, comes into play within each rhetorical situation, namely, constraints. These elements impinge on both those who construct suasive messages and those to whom the messages, the symbolic behaviors, are addressed. Originators of rhetorical acts may also be restricted in terms of resources and ability, but because rhetorical situations tend to recur across time, prior ways of responding place very real boundaries around suasive agents. By way of illustration, anyone delivering a commencement address is constrained, by virtue of all who have done so in the past and by virtue of audience expectations, to recognize and praise the parents and relatives of the graduates. Similarly, it is unthinkable, because of antecedent symbolic behaviors in the same situation, to hold a Fourth of July parade in the United States without featuring the American flag. The power of constraints is extremely real, seldom disregarded or flaunted, and, if so, with considerable consequences. Participants at funeral rituals, no doubt, have heterogenous expectations depending primarily on their prior experience in such activity. These homogeneous expectations cover a wide range of activities (i.e., the corpse *will be* displayed; processions *will* take place; only good things *will be* said about the dead person, etc.).

Rhetorical Situations and Death

The death of an individual, while a natural and real event, brings into existence a rhetorical situation replete with its exigences, audiences, and constraints. Within this rhetorical situation symbolic acts engage audiences in an attempt to bring about multiple changes in those directly and indirectly affected by the death. Those closest to the deceased and therefore most likely to be engulfed in personal grief need rhetorical acts that specifically address their psychological states. If one moves concentrically outward from those most affected into the family, community, or social groups of which the deceased was a member, the rhetorical objectives shift and change. Consolation becomes multifaceted. For some, memories must be recalled; for some, reassurances about future relationships must be offered; for some, new beginnings must be created; for all, the prospect of the inevitability of their own death must be confronted and, to the extent possible, made less ominous. Even the entymology of consolation (*cum* = together; *solari* = to comfort) strikes a disengenuous chord when the multiple social networks of a deceased person are taken into account.

Comforting and alleviating the range of individuals' distress, most certainly, demands a "ritual wrapped in symbolism." Funeral rituals, by definition, can never be successful and certainly not successful in the sense of a lawyer winning a case or a legislator gaining congressional approval of a bill. Funeral rituals, on the contrary, are best not thought of as successful or unsuccessful rhetorical efforts. Consider those most overcome with personal grief. The formal part of most funeral ceremonies lasts a relatively short time, several hours or a few days at most. Intense grief cannot be significantly changed by rhetorical means in that short time. Working through grief requires much time. Yet, would it be accurate to adjudge the ceremony unsuccessful for such persons? Not at all.

Rhetoric has never been, and cannot be, a precise science. That is, the discipline of rhetoric cannot invariably predict that X symbolic behaviors will produce Y effects on Z audience. Rhetoric deals with the contingent, the probable, and what is generally the case.

Better criteria for judging the quality of a funeral ceremony and its symbolic, consolatory behaviors would be appropriateness as perceived by the participants, resistance to innovative change in the ceremony by the community, and a communal sense of rightness or correctness about the rhetorical behaviors used in the ritual. Put in another language frame, the participants in a funeral ritual take part, in varying degrees of activity, both in *creating* and *interpreting* the many symbolic behaviors of the ritual. The merging of speaker/audience, actor/spectator, maker/consumer in a ritual is well expressed by Edmund Leach.

But notice also the contrary aspect of the model. In ordinary culturally defined ritual performance there is no "composer" other than the mythological ancestors. The proceedings follow an ordered pattern which has been established by tradition—"this is our custom." There is usually a "conductor," a master of ceremonies, a chief priest, a central protagonist, whose actions provide the temporal markers for everyone else. But there is no separate audience of listeners. The performers and the listeners are the same people. We engage in rituals in order to transmit collective messages to ourselves.[2]

To the extent that the participants believe that a funeral ritual was proper, fitting, suitable, and right, the rhetorical effort can be said to have fulfilled the exigence of the situation.

A more detailed discussion of the components of a rhetorical situation will reveal the complexity that death creates for rhetorical activity.

At a base level one might claim that all human deaths are the same—biological processes of life end and biological processes of decay begin. Humans, however, are more than an interconnected system of biological processes and, depending on a number of variables, an individual's death will create quite different exigences. The death of an old person, all else being equal, is qualitatively different than the death of a young person. Both will occasion bereavement, grief, and mourning, but the symbolic behaviors used in a consolation ceremony will be adjusted and varied somewhat to deal with the difference. In a similar way the cause of an individual's death—natural and expected versus sudden and violent—are factors in the constellation of variables possible to locate in the rhetorical situation of an individual's death. Similarly, the class and social rank of the deceased are key elements. Drawing upon the earlier work of Robert Hertz who established that individuals possess both a "biological being" and a "social being" that is "grafted onto" a person by others in the society, David Stannard makes this observation: "The death of an important individual thus brings with it serious damage to the social fabric, and a natural and spontaneous effort is then made by the society to compensate for the loss. This is particularly evident in the dramatic funerary rites of smaller, more unified societies where, as Robert Blauner has more recently written, 'much work must be done to restore the social system's functioning.'"[3] Without doubt, a society's statespersons, warriors, and leaders create greater fissures in the societal fabric and consolatory rituals tend to be modified and enlarged accordingly.[4]

The quantitative size of an affected community clearly seems to be a significant variable. As subsequent chapters will illustrate, the symbolic behaviors—verbal, action, and object languages—used in funeral rituals dramatically vary in proportion to the number of people in the social group. Consolatory rituals used in a small Archaic Greek polis, for example, greatly differ in scale from those staged at the death of a Roman Emperor. The death of a person recognized as politically necessary and important for the continuance of one's country occasions uncertainties, fears, and psychic disruptions that differ only in degree from those experienced at the death of a cherished family member.

Religious beliefs, too, come into play at a funeral ritual. The existence and nature of an afterlife, if any, as well as the relationships between god(s) and humans are reflected variously in funeral ceremonies. Emile Durkheim recognized that individuals are connected to the symbolic functioning of their society and a society's symbolic forms are accepted just as the sacred in religious rituals.[5] Extending Durkheim's observation, Eric Rothenbuehler recently concluded that "religious practices, or rites, self-consciously refer to the sacred, protect it, celebrate it, and organize people's attention toward it. Because they bring the individual into contact with the sacred, the religious practices themselves must be set apart in special times and places."[6] Funeral ceremonies in the Classical Era are conspicuous in their spatial and temporal aspects. The Athenian funeral ritual, for example, took place in the winter; ceremonies for Roman aristocrats were held in the Forum. More of this is discussed in the ensuing chapters.

Grief

Another component in the rhetorical exigence of consolation are those most personally affected by the death. The surviving husband, wife, parent, offspring, or longtime intimate friend experience a range and intensity of emotions that the symbolic behaviors in a consolatory ritual dare not overlook but can only address in part. First and foremost among these emotions is grief, the power of which Catherine Sanders describes in these words: "Grief is so impossibly painful, so akin to panic, that ways must be invented to defend against the emotional onslaught of suffering. There is a fear that if one ever gives in fully to grief, one would be swept under—as in a huge tidal wave—never to surface to ordinary emotional states again."[7] An individual experiencing grief may also be experiencing "anger, guilt, physical complaints and illnesses, despair, and sadness."[8] In short, a living organism is influenced by a context of stress which, "if not reversed or compensated for, impairment and damage will result."[9] If the psychological stress caused by the experience of grief, personal and collective, is left unattended, consequences of the most dire sort can happen. Suicide, psychotic response, severe depression, loss of health, or a state of total helplessness do occur if grief is unresolved.[10] Grim as these psychopathologies are for an individual, one can quickly recognize the consequences in a social group if such results took place. Social structures would not only be disrupted but destroyed. "The impact of mortality," Robert Blauner declares, "must be contained."[11] A culture's single most potent "containment practice" is the funeral ritual with its symbolic behaviors, its rhetoric, of consolation. After the initial stage of shock, disbelief, and denial—a phase that is of relatively short duration—anguish and despair occur. Additionally, depending on the existing cultural permissions and prescriptions, weeping, crying, and lamenting accompany the emotions. George Engel claims,

> the wish and need to cry is strong and crying seems to fulfill an important homeostatic function in the work of mourning. In general, crying seems to involve both an acknowledgement of the loss and the regression to a more helpless and childlike status evoked thereby. *In the latter sense crying is a kind of communication.* The grief-stricken person who cries is the recipient of certain kinds of support and help from the group, although this varies greatly in different cultures.[12]

Although the point was made in chapter 1, it bears repeating—the human experience of grief is universal. All humans, regardless of their culture or the century in which they live, experience the emotion of grief and its attendant reactions. The rhetorical situation of a funeral ceremony, in this respect, is the same then as now.

Societal Reactions to Death

Regardless of the culture in question, however, consolatory ceremonies must contain symbolic, suasive behaviors addressed to those living in various states of grief and its attendant manifestations. Typically, the "audience" for a funeral ritual includes more than just the immediate, close survivors. As sociologist Michael Kearl claims, "death's impact ripples not only across acquaintance networks and space but across time as well."[13] Disruption of the equilibrium of social life, unless addressed and remedied, can result in a host of social problems, not the least of which is a debilitating loss of direction and confidence in one's future. Anxiety about future relationships can escalate to damaging levels unless and until social, communal bonds are reestablished and reassured. By way of illustration one can recall William Manchester's description of the communal reaction to the news of President John F. Kennedy's assassination.

> An entire nation had been savaged, and the nation realized it; before the end of the afternoon, when 99.8 percent had learned that the elected president had been murdered the country was in the grip of an extraordinary upheaval. Over half the population wept. Four out of five, in the words of the report, felt "the loss of someone very close and dear," and subsequently nine out of ten suffered "physical discomfort." The discomfort—deep grief—followed confirmation of the president's death. In those first, indecisive thirty minutes there was a dissonant medley of response: dread, hope, prayer, rage, and incredulity.[14]

The elaborate funeral ritual in which an entire nation participated via television did much to reestablish and reassure the national community. Symbolic behaviors showing the orderly transfer of the presidency were featured. Civil and military participation removed doubts about national unity. The visual unity of the Kennedy family—their perceived ability to confront their personal tragedy—was a message for others, the national participants, to do the same. Societal disruption was repaired.

The intensity of human reaction to Kennedy's death was

matched in many ways and exceeded in the outpouring of anger after Martin Luther King's assassination. Stephen Oates, one of King's biographers, recounts that on the day following the murder, "riots flared up in 110 cities, and 39 people were killed, most of them Negroes. More than 75,000 federal troops and National Guardsmen patrolled America's streets. The hardest hit was Washington, D.C. where the fires blazed against the sky and 10 people died."[15] Again, a nation, participating via television, took part in the funeral ceremony, a ceremony greatly different from Kennedy's. Whether or not the symbolic behaviors in Martin Luther King's funeral ceremony aided, in any significant way, in restoring social equilibrium remains arguable.[16]

Quite obviously, not all deaths evoke such manifestations of grief. One could place these instances at the extreme outer end of a continuum, perhaps, and realize that the social disruption accompanying every death graduates downward to less extreme plateaus. The Kennedy and King examples are offered here as contemporary vantage points from which a reader might better understand the symbolic behaviors used at the State funerals for Patroklos in chapter 3 and for Pertinax (A.D. 193), the Roman Emperor in chapter 5. The point remains, nonetheless, that audiences for whom consolatory symbolic behaviors are addressed include individuals experiencing different degrees of disorientation, uncertainty, and insecurity. In a real sense the audience at a consolatory ceremony experiences contradictory and incompatible urges on the one hand to "push the dead away," and, on the other, to "keep the dead alive." Consolatory ceremonies, then, might be viewed as "dramas of disposal" and, simultaneously, a "redefinition of the status of the departed."[17] Although these two notions, at first glance, seem ambivalent if not outright incompatible, Blauner explains the notion of "status transformation" in this way:

> Yet the deceased cannot simply be buried as a dead body: the prospect of total exclusion from the social world would be too anxiety-laden for the living, aware of their own eventual fate. The need to keep the dead alive directs societies to construct rituals that celebrate and ensure a transition to a new social status, that of spirit, a being now believed to participate in a different realm. Thus a

funeral that combines this status transformation with the act of physical disposal is universal to all societies, and has justly been considered one of the crucial *rites de passage*.[18]

These functions are secured, in part, through the constraints on the consolatory ritual itself—that is, the third part of the rhetorical situation.

The Consolatory Ritual

While it might seem self-evident, one of the consequences of an individual's death is the need for a funeral rite with its attendant modes for removing and disposing of the physical remains. From a rhetorical perspective, however, "the ceremonies of the dead affirm the values of the living."[19] While each culture has its own set of beliefs about the nature of death and the afterlife, the physical presence of the dead body and the actuality of the grieving community necessitate action, both real and symbolic, to meet the many demands of the situation. Unlike a more usual rhetorical transaction with a persuader, message, and audience, the funeral ceremony has multiple rhetors. That is, a group of individuals—some with greater, some with lesser responsibilities—engage in the production of the consolatory symbolic behaviors. Unfortunately, the identity of the individuals responsible for conducting and staging funeral ceremonies in ancient times is unknown. In some cases the family, a burial group, or, in a few instances, the state governments were in charge of the rituals. Nonetheless, we know that funerals happened and, accordingly, we can rightfully infer that other humans made the ceremonies happen.

Before proceeding to a more thorough discussion of classical funeral ceremonies—their types, functions, and common elements—an important theoretical issue must be addressed. Put into question form: do the individuals, regardless of culture or historic era, who conduct funeral ceremonies *intend* that various consolatory effects in the audiences occur? Put by way of illustration, does a person who places a bouquet of flowers on a bier intend that some participants in a funeral ceremony will interpret the symbolic behavior to mean: nature contains much that is beautiful and, although we are in the midst of a sorrow-filled funeral, one shall remember that life, too, contains much that is beautiful. The problem of intent has both philosophical and pragmatic dimensions; as such, intent is also central to any rhetorical inquiry.

Philosophically, intent is closely related to questions of causality and moral responsibility. For example, an event happens; someone brings about the event; did that someone intend that the event happen? In the first hypothetical case, a drunk driver kills a pedestrian. Did the driver intend to kill, i.e., possess the silent thought *and* disposition to end the life of another human? In the second case, a philanthropist endows a laser research center that develops a surgical technique responsible for saving the eyesight of thousands of Third World children. Did the philanthropist intend such a result? If so, an affirmative answer is awarded to both of the actors in our hypothetical cases, that is, if we say intent was present in both instances, conceivably and appropriately a gallows might be erected for the driver and a statue for the donor. In these cases the relationship between intent and moral responsibility seems clear. In the first, however, no symbolic behavior was involved; for the second, the philanthropist's large monetary gift can be decoded into the proposition: this person believes science should help people. Conceivably, the decoded proposition, a meaning given to the symbolic behavior by an audience member, could result even if the actual and unknown-to-anyone intent of the giver was to secure an income tax deduction or significantly reduce a spouse's inheritance.

The point of this belabored illustration is that intent of a suasory agent is usually inaccessible to an audience although attributions of intent can be and are made. In any communicative transaction the symbolic behaviors—verbal and other-than-verbal—are accessible to an audience. Interpretations, meanings, and inferences must be drawn on what is present and presented. In the case of a funeral ceremony, laden as they are with cultural caveats and prescriptions, the intent of whoever presents the bouquet of flowers is, for all practical purposes, irrelevant. What matters is the audience's perception of the symbolic behavior and the meaning assigned to the perception.

Does meaning, then, reside only in the "message-audience" matrix? Not at all. Humans both use and assign meanings. In a funeral ceremony, which by its very nature is an unusual, culturally regulated set of procedures each with multiple functions and expected symbolic behaviors, the actual intentions and the attributed intentions of the rhetors do matter. The suasive potentials of the symbolic behaviors both encompass intent and matter greatly. What objectives, then, must these symbolic acts accomplish within the rhetorical situation of a funeral ceremony? What purposes must be served?

In an article, "Death as a Social Practice," Ernest Campbell recognizes a number of functions funeral ceremonies must serve.

> Our common tendency is to perceive grief and funeral practices as oriented toward the past. Someone has departed, and the rites and ceremonies serve the purpose of mourning the dead, reliving the past, reviving treasured memories, honoring the departed who will not return. Certainly this is part of the picture. But a more useful view is to see funeral rites and death attitudes as serving the purpose of assisting the survivors to restructure their relational system. The vital functions of these ceremonies relate really to the future, and not to the past: the restructuring of relationships occasioned by the absence of someone from an established set of relationships.[20]

This Janus-like characteristic—looking both backward and forward, reviewing the past and previewing the future—remains a significant function of funeral ceremonies. In a certain sense, time changes for a funeral ritual; the past and the future become prominently featured while the present becomes irrelevant. Time stops the former life of the deceased—activities, accomplishments, and relationships need to be addressed, retold, and made alive for the community of participants. The deceased becomes the central figure in the cultural drama and a host of symbolic behaviors are directed toward maintaining this centrality. Clothing, decoration, display, position, and the memorial work rhetorically for the audience to recognize the dead person. Past relationships of the deceased, for example, are reenacted by a hierarchical set of culturally enforced behaviors. Those closest to the deceased are located, throughout the ritual, as physically close to the deceased as possible. The surviving father, mother, husband, wife, children, etc., remain in close proximity to the deceased during the wake, the formal ceremony, the various processions and recessions, and the interment. Just as in the deceased's past life relationships ranged from the intimate to the casual, a community in the act of mourning position themselves in such a way as to replicate and reify the most significant aspect of the deceased's former life in the community. Not surprisingly, most of the verbal symbols used in the ritual serve the function of recreating the deceased's past; major portions of a eulogy, for example, or inscriptions on the grave marker both demarcate the individual's prior space in the community, relationships made within the community, and chronological time spent within the group.

Funeral rituals also contain symbolic behaviors that redirect the participants' future. Here, the rhetorical work within a ritual takes on an important, often overlooked, function. In most discursive contexts involving persuasion, audiences recognize that arguments, reasons, and suasory efforts are being directed at them. Admonitions and exhortations to buy, sell, join, contribute, believe, avoid, convict, acquit, or adopt can be countered, modified, or rejected using the available strategies and tactics of argumentative discourse. Confronted with an unwanted persuasive appeal, the ordinary response, for most individuals, is some type of resistance—withdrawal, objection, counter argument, etc. The participants in a funeral ceremony, however, are not subjected to arguments or discursive suasory appeals. Death is a dramatic event calling forth not the forms of reasoned argument but rather dramatic forms of narrative, poetry, and theater. The ordinary response to these forms is acceptance, agreement, internalization, and participation. These forms persuade in the sense that the moral behavior of the characters in a drama offers the participating audience models for believing and acting, for assimilating values, and for living one's life.

The symbolic behaviors in a funeral ritual that affect participants' future lives can best be labeled *epideictic*. In subsequent chapters more detail about epideictic rhetoric will be presented. For now, one need only understand the term to signify rhetoric that occurs on a special occasion. People create occasions for a multitude of purposes: to celebrate, to commemorate, to honor, to dedicate, to mourn, etc. Each type of special occasion has its own character; its identifying ethos circumscribing and, to a considerable extent, controlling those who participate in the occasion. Birthday celebrations possess an ethos of festive giving; funerals, an ethos of solemn reflection. Immersed in such an ethos, those participating in a funeral ritual become susceptible to the instrumentality of the symbolic behaviors. The funeral ritual provides abundant opportunities for self-reflection—listening, watching, and quietly moving. Confronted with irrefutable evidence of mortality, one is predisposed to project and identify. Hearing the deceased praised can stir a resolve to emulate and imitate. Moving in unison with other participants one is compelled to accept the fact that each person is not only separate and individual but also united in a bond of community. The ritual provides opportunities for social interaction; relationships can be recognized, renewed, and restructured at the typical gathering before the formal ceremony or at the customary funeral meal. The epideictic nature of the ritual clearly functions to influence the future lives of the participants.

Yet another equally important function is the *rite de passage*: for the dead a move to "another, perhaps eternal, system of role relationships";[21] for the survivors, a transition to a changed set of relationships. More specifically, funeral ceremonies function to "announce to the community that the bereaved are now in a new and unaccustomed status, and that normal role performance is not to be expected from them for awhile."[22] Funeral ceremonies also function to keep communities intact which is one reason the cultural admonition not to speak ill of the dead retains both currency and strength. Pillorying a flawed life works against reintegrating a communal group.

Funeral ceremonies function to enact the outer boundary of bereavement for a community. Campbell, for example, claims "it is probable also that a rational, secular, efficiency-oriented society produces norms that encourage early termination of a mourning attitude."[23] In later chapters we will encounter numerous instances in which Greco-Roman speakers and writers urge an appropriate boundary for expressions of mourning. No social organization, if it is to both continue functioning productively and maintaining itself effectively can afford the debilitating impact of a prolonged bereavement.

Although it may seem paradoxical to state, in a certain sense one can claim that a funeral ceremony does not end with the disposition of the physical remains. The cemetery—taken here in an extended sense to include the place *where* the remains are ultimately located, i.e., tomb, mausoleum, ossuary, etc.—and the symbolic behaviors of consolation that occur therein serve a different set of functions. Of cemeteries in general W. Lloyd Warner observes that "the cemetery reflects many of the community's basic beliefs about what kind of society it is, what the persons of men are, where each fits or is fitted into the secular world of the living and the spiritual society of the dead."[24] The cemetery does not end in the sense that a formal ceremony ends. Monuments, art work, and location all serve to reunite the living and the dead long after grief, mourning, and bereavement have ended. One might profitably view a funeral ceremony, then, as a sequence or set of movements in which disassociation functions are provided. The dead are separated from the living. Then, an associative function is provided. The living are rebonded, regrouped, and reintegrated. The cemetery, however, offers the synthesis, the reuniting, of the living with the dead who live, not in a physical sense, but in a psychological one of memory. "The cemetery locates the dead in time and space, thus maintaining their reality to those who wish to continue relations with them."[25] As symbolic behaviors the rhetorical impact of cemeteries dare not be dismissed. Gravestones, sarcophagi, vaults, temples, and mausoleums work rhetorically as memorials, records, repetitions, or continuations for those most affected by the death and also for those unable to participate. The scale and scope of many Greco-Roman funeral monuments (e.g., the "tombs" of Augustine and Hadrian) can be construed as visual messages, grand to be sure, offering an almost impervious command to reunite observers with the deceased.[26] The dead remain symbolically alive in cemeteries.

We turn now to a closer analysis of the symbolic behaviors of consolation used in the Classical Era.

NOTES

1. Lloyd F. Bitzer, "The Rhetorical Situation," *Philosophy and Rhetoric* 1 (1968): 1–14. In his words:

> to say that rhetoric is situational means: (1) rhetorical discourse comes into existence as a response to situation, in the same sense that an answer comes into existence in response to a question, or a solution in response to a problem; (2) a speech is given rhetorical significance by the situation, just as a unit of discourse is given significance as answer or as solution by the question or problem; (3) a rhetorical situation must exist as a necessary condition of rhetorical discourse, just as a question must exist as a necessary condition of an answer; (4) many questions go unanswered and many problems remain unsolved; similarly, many rhetorical situations mature and decay without giving birth to rhetorical utterance; (5) a situation is rhetorical insofar as it needs and invites discourse capable of participating with situation and thereby altering its reality; (6) discourse is rhetorical insofar as it functions (or seeks to function) as a fitting response to a situation which needs and invites it. (7) Finally, the situation controls the rhetorical response in the same sense that the question controls the answer and the problem controls the solution. Not the rhetor and not persuasive intent, but the situation is the source and ground of rhetorical activity—and, I should add, of rhetorical criticism. (6–7)

2. Leach, *Culture and Communication*, 45.
3. David E. Stannard, "Introduction," in *Death in America*, ed. David E. Stannard, x (College Park, PA: Pennsylvania State University Press, 1975). See also Robert Blauner, "Death and Social Structure," *Psychiatry* 29 (1966): 387.
4. Each of the several branches of the Armed Services in the United States, for example, uses their own *Manual for Conducting Military Funerals*. While one can observe a certain semi-fixed set of ritualized and symbolic activities for those at all ranks, the deaths of higher ranking officers tend to be accorded more expansive ceremonies than enlisted individuals. For example, the participants at the funeral of an Airman First Class would not see airplanes in the "missing man" formation at the interment; if the deceased were a colonel, perhaps; if the deceased were a general, without doubt. See for the specifics of the rubrics, AFR 143–1(C5), 31 March 81, ch. 16, "Military Honors and Conduct of Funerals."

Also *The Navy Funeral Manual*, S/N 0500–LP–277–8243, Rev. 1986, with this statement of purpose: "Our nation regards the burying of its military dead as a solemn and sacred obligation. Ancient naval and military customs are the basis for honors at their funerals. The flag covering the casket symbolizes their service in the armed forces of the United States. Taps are played to mark the beginning of the last, long sleep and to express hope and confidence in an ultimate reveille to come. According to ancient belief, the three volleys that are fired were to scare away evil spirits. Today they are fired out of respect for the deceased member's service to his/her country. To signify that at death all persons are equal, the honorary pallbearers are positioned in reserve order of rank" (i).

5. Emile Durkheim, *The Elementary Forms of the Religious Life*, trans. J. W. Swain (New York: The Free Press, 1965).

6. Eric W. Rothenbuehler, "Values and Symbols in Orientations to the Olympics," *Critical Studies in Mass Communication* 6 (1989): 140–41.

7. Catherine M. Sanders, *Grief: The Mourning After: Dealing With Adult Bereavement* (New York: John Wiley and Sons, 1989), 9. See also Elizabeth Kubler-Ross, *On Death and Dying* (New York: MacMillan Publishing Co., 1969); C. S. Lewis, *A Grief Observed* (New York: The Seabury Press, 1961); Lily Pincus, *Death in the Family* (New York: Pantheon Press, 1974); B. Raphael, *The Anatomy of Bereavement* (London: The Hutchinson Publishing Co., 1984); R. Schulz, *The Psychology of Death, Dying, and Bereavement* (Reading, MA: Addison-Wesley Publishing Co., 1974); G. M. Vernon, *The Sociology of Death: An Analysis of Death-Related Behavior* (New York: The Ronald Press, 1970).

8. Sanders, *Grief*, 10. In a similar vein, Jackson describes the emotion in this way, "Grief is a complex emotion. It is always personal. It is an extension of the inner life of a grieving individual. It reflects his values and his inner strength and weakness. It is significant behavior at a time when inner stress may be so great that other alternatives for managing life crises become inoperative." Edgar N. Jackson, *The Many Faces of Grief* (Nashville, TN: The Abingdon Press, 1977), 11.

9. George F. Engel, *Psychological Development in Health and Disease* (Philadelphia, PA: W. B. Saunders Co., 1962), 272.

10. Engel, *Psychological Development*, 279ff.

11. Blauner, "Death," 379ff.

12. Engel, *Psychological Development*, 275.

13. Michael C. Kearl, *Endings: A Sociology of Death and Dying* (New York: Oxford University Press, 1989), 67.

14. William Manchester, *The Death of a President: November 20–November 25, 1963* (New York: Harper and Rowe Publishers, 1967), 189.
15. Stephen B. Oates, *Let the Trumpet Sound: The Life of Martin Luther King, Jr.* (New York: The New American Library, 1982), 494.
16. David L. Lewis, *King: A Biography*, 2d ed. (Urbana, IL: University of Illinois Press, 1978), 391. Lewis' extended account of the mule cart used to transport the body, the untalented singers at Morehouse College, the inept eulogy, and the abortive failure of the anthem, "We Shall Overcome," clearly indicate that the funeral ritual was not appropriate for Mr. Lewis and, quite possibly, for many others.
17. Blauner, "Death," 387.
18. Blauner, "Death," 387.
19. Ernest Q. Campbell, "Death as a Social Practice," in *Perspectives on Death*, ed. Liston O. Mills, 229 (New York: Abingdon Press, 1969).
20. Campbell, "Death," 215.
21. Campbell, "Death," 218.
22. Campbell, "Death," 219.
23. Campbell, "Death," 223.
24. W. Lloyd Warner, *The Living and the Dead* (New Haven: Yale University Press, 1959), 280.
25. Campbell, "Death," 228.
26. The best single source, to my knowledge, on this subject is James Stevens Curl, *A Celebration of Death: An Introduction to Some of the Buildings, Monuments, and Settings of Funerary Architecture in the Western European Tradition*, (New York: Charles Scribner's Sons, 1980). See J. W. Day, "Rituals in Stone: Early Greek Epigrams and Monuments," *The Journal of Hellenic Studies* 109 (1989):16–28. Also John Van Sickle, "The Elogia of the Cornelii Scipiones and the Origin of Epigram at Rome," *American Journal of Philology* 108 (1987):41–55.

Chapter Three

The Archaic Greek Funeral

Precisely how the funerals of ordinary individuals in early Greece were conducted is not known with much certainty. As with most primitive, superstitious cultures one can confidently assume that a person's death occasioned grief and fear, that cremation or inhumation were employed, and that an individual's clan developed some sort of bereavement code of behavior.

That such was the case in Archaic Greece (750 B.C.–500 B.C.) is attested to by both literary and archaeological evidence. Accordingly, in this chapter, both sources of evidence will be used to recreate the instrumental, symbolic behaviors used in the funeral ceremony.

The Homeric Funeral

One can turn to the description of funeral behaviors in Homer's *Iliad* to learn what was done and what the rhetorical potentials and functions of the behaviors were in Archaic Greece. An objection can be raised insofar as the *Iliad* is an account of warrior-kings and not an account of the ways ordinary people in the general population lived and died. Since the *Iliad* served as the idealized pattern on which later Greeks lived their lives, one can gain, nonetheless, some insight into the probable practices. In *Homer and His Influence*, John Scott asserts:

> With Homer Greek culture began, with him it flourished, with him it won dominion, with him it fell, and with him it rose again. He was the first adequately to express the Hellenic spirit and he was the last to keep it alive. No other great people has been so much the creation of a single person, and he was to the Greeks their law-giver, teacher, and poet, combining in himself the characters of Moses, David, and the prophets.[1]

Some small measure of the unquestioned authority Homer held for the Greeks—and held for centuries—is partially contained in the statement that Homer was the "Bible of the Greeks." More compelling, perhaps, is the fact that Aeschines during a court case in the fourth century B.C., many centuries after Homer composed the *Iliad*, could turn to a law clerk and ask that he recite twenty-six verses from memory.[2] Knowledge of Homer was simply a safely assumed fact of life. Whether or not this long-lasting knowledge of Homer directly influenced the way funerals were conducted cannot be resolved satisfactorily. Proof for such claims does not exist except by the abundance of similarities between the funeral rituals in Homer and those of later centuries. The mourners, marches, laments, games, and cremation practices used after Homer bear a remarkable likeness to those described in the *Iliad*.

The funeral episodes in the *Iliad* reveal much about what was culturally expected; the symbolic behaviors also indicate the suasive functions of each. A compressed description, then, needs to precede a close rhetorical analysis.

In Book 18 of the *Iliad*,[3] Nestor announces the death of Patroklos to Achilleus: "You must hear from me the ghastly message of a thing I wish never had happened. Patroklos has fallen, and now they are fighting over his body which is naked" (18–21). Consistent with the earlier discussion of grief (chapter 2), Achilleus physically reacts to the message: "In both hands he caught up the grimy dust, and poured it over his head and face, and fouled his handsome countenance, and the black ashes were scattered over his immortal tunic. And he himself mightily in his might, in the dust lay at length, and took and tore at his hair with his hands, and defiled it" (23–27). After the body had been recovered from the battlefield, handmaidens, members of the immediate households, "stricken at heart cried out aloud, and came running out of doors about valiant Achilleus, and all of them beat their breasts with their hands, and the limbs went slack in each of them" (29–32).

As the story progresses the Achaians, the community to which the deceased Patroklos belonged, "mourned all night in lamentation" (315). Achilleus, Patroklos' battle comrade, confidant, and close friend speaks a lament in which the death is viewed as an event attributable as much to the gods as to the enemy warrior. Then preparations are made to attend to the physical remains: "But when the water had come to a boil in the shining bronze, then they washed the body and annointed it softly with olive oil and stopped the gashes in his body with stored up unguents and laid him on a bed, and, shrouded him in a thin sheet from head to foot, and covered that over with a white mantle" (349–353). Lamentations, a reader learns, continued throughout the night.[4]

A problem of interpretation arises in Book 19. Achilleus elected to abstain from food and drink although the rest of his warrior community did not. Whether or not fasting was an expected behavior in the bereavement ritual for Homeric Greeks or whether the self-imposed "penance" can better be read as a plot mechanism to highlight the intensity of the hero's eagerness for revenge is difficult to determine. While avoiding food is certainly consonant with recognized responses to grief, no one else in Achilleus' community apparently engaged in such mortification of the flesh. The point is worthy of note, however, if for no other reason than to underscore the difficulty of using dramatic forms of language for other-than-intended purposes. In cases where some action may or may not have been part of a socially recognized component of the funeral ceremony, caution and conservatism favor a judgment of omission.

Two laments, clearly part of the ritual, are addressed—one public, the second more private. Briseis, a young woman earlier captured in a siege by Achilleus, only to be taken away by Agamemnon and returned at the death of Patroklos, after seeing the dead body "folded him in her arms cried shrilly above him and with her hands tore at her breasts and her soft throat and beautiful forehead" (283–285). In her laments Briseis recalls the dead warrior's promise that she would one day marry Achilleus and remembers his many kindnesses (297–300). Then, after sending his soldiers away, Achilleus himself recalls past favors and expresses sorrow for his father, his son, and himself (315–337). The next day, after killing Hektor, the Trojan warrior who had killed Patroklos, Achilleus called his comrades and charioteers together (23.5ff.) and issued a command: "We must drive close up to Patroklos and mourn him, since such is the privilege of the perished" (23.8–9). This done the warriors prepare a feast and Achilleus, again refusing to wash, issues a most revealing command:

> No, before Zeus, who is the greatest of gods and the high-
> est, there is no right in letting water come near my head,
> until I have laid Patroklos on the burning pyre, and
> heaped the mound over him, and cut my hair for him,
> since there will come no second sorrow like this to my
> heart again while I am still one of the living. Then let us
> now give way to the gloomy feast; and with the dawn cause
> your people to rise, o lord of men Agamemnon, and bring
> in timber and lay it by, with all that is fitting for the dead
> man to have when he goes down under the gloom and the
> darkness, so that with the more speed the unwearying fire
> may burn him away from our eyes and the people turn
> back to that which they must do. (23.43–53)

Later that night the ghost of Patroklos appears to Achilleus and asks for his "rite of burning" (23.76) and asks that, in due time, his ashes be buried with those of Achilleus.[5] Achilleus grants the request and, the following morning, the funeral pyre is built and a military parade takes place. Each warrior adds a lock of his hair to the corpse (23.135–137), animals are slaugh-tered and added to the pyre, jars of oil and honey are placed on the pyre, Achilleus offers prayers to the gods (23.160–197), and the fire is lit. As an important part of the ritual, the fire burns for a time and is then extinguished. The remains of Patroklos are placed in a "golden jar" (23.243), and buried in a "fitting grave mound" (23.245–6).[6]

Joyful festivities immediately followed the burial. Prizes[7] were awarded in a number of contests: chariot racing (360ff.), boxing (657ff.), wrestling (700ff.), foot racing (740ff.), sword fighting (810ff.), weight throwing (826ff.), archery, and spear throwing. With the end of the last event the funeral ritual for Patroklos ended.

Granted, the symbolic behaviors in the Homeric account are those of a warrior class consisting of feudal warlords. Granted also, Homer's account contains no hint about the rep-resentativeness or nonrepresentatives of this funeral ceremony for a military leader killed in battle. Nonetheless, the account must have contained some verisimilitude otherwise the audiences who, for centuries, attended recitals of the epic would have seriously questioned or objected to the description. Moreover, the description of the funeral ritual in Homer bears a striking resemblance to that of the ceremony used in Archaic Classical Greece. Margaret Alexiou's systematic account of the actual procedures used in the Greek funeral[8] divides them into three phases: the wake, the funeral procession, and the burial.

Phases of the Archaic Greek Funeral

After a person died, preparation of the body took place almost immediately. Although in later centuries the ritual was held indoors, initially, it took place out-of-doors to facilitate the participation of community, most of whom would take part. Typically the women of the household were responsible for closing the eyes and mouth, washing and anointing the body, and then draping a white cloth over it. Positioning of the body was a significant part of the preparation. Placed on a bier with the feet pointed away from the dwelling, the body rested atop a covered mattress. Then, decorations were added. "Sometimes it (the body) was strewn with wild marjoram, celery and other herbs, believed to ward off evil spirits, then laid on vine, myrtle, or laurel leaves. The head, which at this stage was uncovered was decorated with garlands of laurel and celery. At the door stood a bowl of water brought from outside for the purification of all who came into contact with the corpse, and ointment vessels were placed under the bier."[9] From the time of Homer to the fifth century, according to evidence derived from vase paintings, this part of the ritual apparently did not change significantly. When the preparation of the body was complete, the wake could begin.

At the site of public visitation, positioning of the members of the funeral drama again becomes important. A male, usually the father, welcomed guests but stood away from the displayed body. The closest female member of the family stood at the head of the corpse with other female mourners stood alongside. Males, with right arms raised, moved by in procession during which time "the chief mourner usually clasps the head of the dead man with both hands, while the others may try to touch his hand, their own right hand stretched over him."[10]

Gestures and sounds were part of the ceremony. "The violent tearing of the hair, face, and clothes were not acts of uncontrolled grief, but part of the ritual indispensable to lamentation throughout antiquity."[11] Lamentations were sung and often accompanied by reed-pipe music. The mourners apparently moved in rhythm, a type of dance, as the lamentations were sung in antiphonal modes.[12]

After several days of this public visitation, usually three, the ceremony moved to the burial site. The order of march was an integral and highly public part of the ritual. The bier was "carried on a wagon and drawn by two horses, followed by kinswomen, professional mourners, and armed men."[13] Wailing and ritual laments also occurred during this phase of the ceremony. This phase typically was of short duration.

At the tomb, offerings were made of locks of hair, garlands, and clothing; libations were poured; and various food stuffs (e.g., milk, honey, fruit, etc.) were placed atop the dead body. Animals were sacrificed and burnt over the grave and, later, torches and lamps were placed near the grave site. When the burial was completed, the home and those most closely associated with the deceased were purified and, then, all the deceased's relatives joined in a meal. Grave markers were added at a later date.

Archaic Laments

One would expect those most overcome with grief to express the emotion not only in other-than-verbal languages but in words, lamentations, as well. A most curious and, simultaneously, most telling addition to the Archaic use of laments did involve the use of professional, unrelated to the deceased, mourners. During the funeral ceremony these professional singers served as a type of collectivized leader for the stylized expressions of grief that were apparently believed to be a necessary part of the ceremony. That two distinct groups of lament-makers were used is attested to again by Homer.

In the last book of the *Iliad*, when Hektor's body is returned to be prepared for burial, the reader is told: "They laid him on a carved bed, and seated beside him the singers who were to lead the melody in the dirge, and the singers chanted the song of sorrow, and the women were mourning beside them" (24.719–723). Homer does not provide the words used by these "singers," instead he includes the laments of the three women closest to the deceased: Andromache, his wife; Hekabe, his mother; and Helen, his sister-in-law. Each expressed an individualized, highly personal sorrow. Andromache is bitter at the bleak prospect for their son's future and pained at the manner of his death. Hekabe grieves that she has lost her favorite son. Helen weeps because she has lost a most protective friendship. These personal expressions of grief, however, were apparently a type of choral reply to the language and melodies used by the professional mourners.

Precisely what the professionals sang is somewhat uncertain; however, poets did compose choral laments for pay in the sixth century B.C. One such poet, Simonides (ca. 556–468), at the deaths of a Thessalian ruling family, composed a funeral dirge, a fragment of which follows: "If tho be'st a mortal man, never say what tomorrow will bring, nor when thou seest a man happy, how long he shall be happy. For swift is change—nay, not so swift the changing course of the wide-winged fly."[14] Although direct evidence is clearly insufficient to warrant an accurate depiction of an actual, antiphonal interplay between the professional mourners and the spontaneous laments of the next of kin, the fact that such a choral exchange took place is certain.

Highly speculative though it be, one can envision a scene in which the professional mourners might sing something like a stylized thematic prompt which, in turn, could either be answered and amplified by the next of kin or, if no answering lament were forthcoming, simply provide an appropriate answering lament and recycle the pattern. Devotional chants sung responsively as part of a liturgy by two choirs are not unknown even at present. The rhetorical functions of this dual approach to funeral lamentation will be discussed later. As an instrumental symbolic behavior, however, the several kinds of lament are obviously directed and addressed to a community, the *polis*, and it is to this dimension of the funeral ceremony that we now turn.

The Polis

In his book, *Burial and Ancient Society*, Ian Morris makes the following observation about the Greek polis: "The Greeks invented politics, and made political relationships the core of the form of state which they called the polis. The essence of the polis' ideal was the identity of the citizens with the state itself . . . all authority was located in the community. . . . The polis' powers were total: there were no natural rights of the individual, sanctioned by a higher authority. . . . The citizens were the state."[15]

Conventionally, early Greek history is usually divided into the Dark Ages (ca. 1100–700 B.C.), the Archaic Period (ca. 750–500 B.C.), and the Classical Era (ca. 500–300 B.C.). Precisely when the polis as a political institution began is both moot and not necessary for this study. No doubt early forms were existent in the late Dark Ages and the early Archaic Period, the approximate time that Homer's *Iliad* was compiled. During this time, extended families, ruled by the eldest, joined together in villages. The next stage in the probable evolutionary development was the polis, a state about which Aristotle observes: "The complete community of several villages is the polis, which has already almost reached the level of self-sufficiency, and having come into existence for the sake of life, it exists for the good life."[16]

Most city-states were geographically small, some covering only 170 square kilometers. Athens, the polis from which the bulk of our extant evidence derives was among the largest, encompassed 2,400 square kilometers. Only adult males could take part in the political decisions of the polis; women, children, slaves, and foreigners, although active contributors to the economy of the institution, were excluded from political affairs. "Most poleis had a central town with markets, temples and a fortified acropolis, although the bulk of the population would usually live in villages."[17] As is the case with all communities, differences in wealth based on property ownership spawned an aristocratic group who, in turn, tended to exert influence of various sorts in the political machinations of the polis. A death in such a city-state would be disruptive for all its citizens. A modern reader will note a most curious absence. There is no eulogy, no funeral oration, no one addressing the community about the virtues of the deceased, no offering of consolatory sentiments, nor is there any explaining of the role of the supernatural in the affairs of mortals. Why no eulogy?

Members of the polis—relatively small in number; living in a preliterate, oral culture; generally well known to each other—probably did not need a public eulogy. Perhaps their beliefs in the relationships between humans and the after life was such that fulfilling their religious activities—polluting, cleansing, offering sacrifice, etc.—would be sufficient. Despite the fact that no formal systematization of persuasive discourse existed in Archaic Greece, the symbolic behaviors used in the funeral ceremonies were used rhetorically to effect suasory ends. How these behaviors functioned rhetorically is the topic to which we now turn.

Symbolic Behavior and Rhetorical Function

Rites of passage have a tripartate structure: separation, marginalization, and aggregation.[18] All three involve relationships: previous social roles break, then shift into an altered state, and then those involved in the rite enter into a new, stable relationship. Funerals, as rites of passage, can be analyzed using these three phases as primary, overarching purposes within which symbolic behaviors are used. As is true with any set of descriptive categories, or phases, these are neither discrete nor rigidly demarcated, but instead are dynamic. That is, symbolic behaviors of separation, for example, can and do extend into the aggregation phase of the funeral rite. Table 3.1 displays the three phases of the funeral ritual with the symbolic behaviors and elements of each.

At a general level one can see displayed within the three phases of the funeral rite of passage the symbolic behaviors, verbal and other-than-verbal, and the elements of these behaviors. A number of these features, however, merit further development.

Separation

Announcing

Events that are threatening to a community require an agreed upon, unequivocal signal. A whistle, siren, trumpet, or

TABLE 3.1
SYMBOLIC BEHAVIORS IN THE ARCHAIC FUNERAL

Phases (Purposes) of the Rite	Symbolic Behaviors	Elements
I. Separation		
	1. Announcing	—directive language
	2. Refiguring:	
	a. the living	—befouling and marring actions
	b. the dead	—beautifying and adorning actions
	3. Lamenting	
	a. Personal	—individualized expressions of loss
	b. Professional	—cultural themes of mortality
II. Marginalization		
	1. Parading	
	a. Military	—massed maneuvers executed with precision
	b. Civilian	—individual movement with culturalized gestures
	2. Ceremonial Marching	—culturized placement —culturized rhythm
	3. Lamenting	—song
III. Aggregation		
	1. Burying	
	a. Placement of grave goods	—material objects of the deceased —material objects of the community
	b. Display of interment apparatus	—size of pyre and grave mound —quality of container for remains
	2. Lamenting	
	3. Celebrating	—physical activities —communal meal

flag is often used as a device after cueing a knowledgeable participant about a significant change. Death requires a verbal announcement because it is too important to rely on other-than-verbal systems. Why so?

The verbal announcement of a death in a community serves a number of rhetorical functions including a call to preparedness and the identification of the deceased. A member of a community, especially a small, closely interconnected and interdependent one, needs to know *who* died and not simply that someone in their community died. Rhetorically, the announcement functions in context as a single premise enthymeme. That is, to learn that "*X* has died" requires each affected member of a community to link individual and collective premises to the announcement. A given individual, for instance, could adduce a highly personal chain of implications: (pragmatic) "*X* was going to loan me money," "Now I have nowhere to turn," or (affiliative) "*X* was my closest friend," "*X* will not be there when I need her ever again," etc.

Apart from these hypothetical and individual premises, shared community beliefs also come into play as part of the enthymeme. At its simplest level, "*X* has died," "My family will be expected to be part of the ceremony," "We must prepare to go," etc.

The announcement of an individual's death serves other purposes as well. By such an announcement, audiences, or members of a polis for instance, would be influenced to identify their own mortality and eventual death with that of the deceased. These audiences are influenced to change roles and adopt, temporarily, behaviors accepted and expected by the funeral ritual. That is, the announcement itself calls forth an individual's experiences with the about to be enacted ritual and these prior experiences warrant a sequence of changes—garment choice, selection of grave goods, wake protocols, etc.

Finally, an announcement of death functions to introduce an audience to the dual themes of the funeral ritual. Much like a standard introduction to a speech, an audience's attention and mind set is focused on the life/death opposition and the communal drama that is the funeral rite complete with all its various participants and set into an inexorable motion. It is at this point that separation begins.

Refiguring

Nowhere is the juxtaposition of opposing elements of symbolic behavior more apparent and easily discerned than here. To separate the deceased from the living, diametrically opposed role reversals predominate. As was amply illustrated in the review of the Archaic Greek funeral (and, it is worth noting the same will be true for the Roman funeral ceremony as well) the living and the dead are oppositionally refigured into an array of action and object languages. The corpse is cleaned and beautified. The living are dirtied and marred. The corpse is unblemished; the living are disfigured. The corpse is anointed; the living are unwashed. The corpse is draped and covered; the living have ripped and torn raiment. The corpse is displayed at rest; the living are agitated and frenetic. The corpse is touched affectionately; the living receive no reciprocating gestures. The corpse is silent; the living are loud.

The corpse is presented to the living in as amplified and lifelike a configuration as possible. The reclining, restful posture argues graphically for the tranquility of the death condition. No doubt the ablutions, grooming, anointing, and clothing in white work as a persuasive message of invitation. Even if the fact of death cannot yet be accepted, the appearance of the corpse in death cannot be rejected. How best, then, to explain the symbolic behaviors of the living?

If separation is the initial goal of the funeral ritual, identification with the deceased must be avoided. The symbolic behaviors of refiguring of the living and the elements of disfigurement and debasement can be read as messages amplifying the pain and anguish of death both for the close familial survivors and the community at large. Just as death is fear provoking, the pulling of hair, scratching of face, rending of garments, and befouling of body can elicit emotions of fear they can also denote the tumult, confusion, and disintegration death has caused in the community. Viewed from this perspective death is anything but inviting and attractive. Admittedly, some of these behaviors may properly be expressive of personal grief rather than instrumental and rhetorical. That such is the case would be reasonable and, probably, incontrovertible. Yet, from an audience perspective—those participants in the ritual not *in extremis*—meanings other than personal grief can be assigned these behaviors. The enormity of the loss, for example, can be construed as too immense and too overwhelming for words, expressive or instrumental, to adequately cope. Elements used by the living to refigure themselves serve, then, as suasive messages to others in the community to not expect the usual modes of interaction. Death, indeed, may render words inadequate but the actions of one stricken with grief can suasively control one's communal associates. The symbolic behaviors of the living, bizarre though they might seem to a modern reader, are, after all, messages sent by the living to the living. Survival and maintenance of the community overcomes the departure of the deceased. Confronted with this juxtaposition of choices the need to separate from the deceased becomes persuasive.

Lamenting

One can see from Table 3.1 that ritualized lamentation continues through all three phases of the funeral ceremony: separation, marginalization, and aggregation. Enough has already been said about the several types of oppositions used in this symbolic behavior—personal vis-à-vis paid professional, leader vis-à-vis antiphonal chord reply. Clearly, opposition is present but why the lengthy span through all three phases? Typically, burial took place three days after death and, without a doubt, wealthier families might employ more professional mourners than others as a status gesture. But note, lamenting does not directly serve any one of the three purposes of the ritual. Can it serve any rhetorical functions?

Without a record of what was actually sung by way of funeral lamentation, it is hard to analyze the rhetorical functions. The schedule for the laments, however, offers a reasonable interpretation. Lamentations serve the suasory function of reinforcing the solemnity of the ritual for community members who enter, participate, and leave the ceremony at different times. Since not all of the people in a community would be, or could be, for that matter, present at the preparation of the body, it is reasonable to assume that some would come to view the body later. Similarly, since the vital work of a community cannot come to a complete and total halt for three days it is reasonable to assume that some, conceivably, would be in the ceremonial march or at the burial but not at both. An extended lament, then, can serve to denote separation from one's companion even for those joining the ritual for the first time at the aggregation phase.

Extending the lamentation up to but not beyond the actual interment or cremation serves other rhetorical functions as well. Not the least of these functions is that of controlling communal grief. An audience, hearing the words, melody, and antiphonal arrangement of the lament are enabled to use the expressions of loss and sorrow as their own thereby diminishing the opportunity for explosive and spontaneous eruptions of anguish, eruptions capable of provoking widespread and destructive consequences.[19] Messages of control also play a significant role in the marginalization phase.

Marginalization

Parading

As indicated early in this chapter, the Archaic Greek funeral involved both a military parade and what can be termed a "civilian" parade—the stylized movements and gestures used by those who come to visit the corpse. A military parade at a funeral can be interpreted in numerous ways, most commonly as an activity honoring the dead person's prior service. The Greek warriors parading past the body of Patroklos can be viewed as "paying their respects," or "saying farewell" in a military modality. After all, any military group develops its own protocols of group behavior to maintain cohesion, unity, discipline, and courage.

During the middle phase of the rite, marginalization, an abnormal social condition prevails. The body of the deceased is physically present, a visual reminder of the social person who once was alive and is no longer. In the religious belief of the pre-Classical Greeks, the body had to be buried before the soul could enter the underworld. Superstition may well have motivated some of the preburial behaviors. Even so, the members of a polis, traumatized by the death of one of their own, would experience emotional ambiguities of considerable proportion, fear and vulnerability the most prominent. A military parade interjected within such a socio-emotional context is a distinct message affording security from the threat of harm. The inse-curities prompted and occasioned by the death and the physical presence of death are juxtaposed with a visual exhibition of potential protection, strength, and safeguarding. The immobil-ity and helplessness of the deceased are placed in opposition to the demonstrative mobility and projected power of a collective in a military parade.

During marginalization all relationships are in flux. The social order, the status of the dead person, and the polis itself is undergoing change. These elements are set against a defin-ing characteristic of both a military parade and the stylized movements used by members of a polis as they approached to view the body of the deceased. Both are executed with preci-sion, more pronounced in military displays, perhaps, than in the more individualized movement to the bier. Precision, how-ever, is an essential counterpoint to the indeterminate and in-definite status of a grieving polis. Why so?

Precision is necessary when one cannot afford the conse-quences of inexactness. Examples of such consequences are easily adduced: architectural disasters, inappropriate medica-tions, flaws in accounting, and military defeat. Precision en-sures predictability; precision both controls and is controlling. At the very phase in a funeral ceremony when, in a manner of speaking, the dead are not yet dead and the living are not yet alive again, the reassuring presence of precision acts rhetori-cally to restrain an otherwise unpredictable situation from to-tally self-destructing.

Marginalization begins to blend somewhat toward the final phase of aggregation with the collective movement, the cere-monial march, but social roles are still reversed and social status of the participants is still uncertain. A reversal of hier-archy contains the suasory messages in the ceremonial funeral march.

Ceremonial Marching

Alongside the laying out portion of the ritual, the funeral procession to the burial site was the most lavish. "Files of danc-ing women, armed soldiers and chariots, and mourners,"[20] are regularly depicted on vase paintings from the era. Leading the ceremonial procession was the "bier carried on a wagon and drawn by two horses."[21] The ceremonial march, more akin to a collective dance than a tightly regimented military maneuver, is rich with symbolic behavior. Again, elements within the enactment of these behaviors are placed in opposition to serve, rhetorically, as suasive messages to the community.

The march itself, a communal action, contrasts with the passive repose of the deceased. All those engaged in the ceremonial march perform their several roles on the ground; the deceased has not touched the earth since the body was prepared for display. The dead body is carried by machinery and animals; the society carries itself. The dead lead and the living follow. In such a condition the corpse is clearly in a state of transition, or of marginalization. For the time being the deceased is neither with the living, of the earth, or in the earth. Nor, for that matter are the living yet separated from the deceased, since the physical remains are very much in evidence.[22] As a march the key participants engage in a reciprocal and oppositional movement; the deceased is moved to a final location while the community makes the same movement and returns.

The acting community both gives and receives multiple messages in this phase of the ritual. Moving together toward the site of the burial reaffirms the potency of the collective. Grief, personal in nature, is contrasted with, shared among, and mitigated by the physical and dancelike behavior of the living. To denote the transitional status of the deceased, the body is treated differently than the bodies of the participants, who remain essentially as they were prior to the death. Those with specialized functions in the society, singers and warriors, for example, assume their roles in the ceremonial march to assert the permanence of the living group. Messages of separation can be read in the order of the march. Although the corpse is in the lead position, the corpse does not lead, initiate, or set the pace. The community, in effect, shares the leadership function by configuring the procession as if the dead person were in command or in charge. While the fact of death cannot be controlled, the consequences clearly can be. In the ceremonial march the social roles of follower and leader appear one way in reality; however, at the symbolic behavioral level the living guide themselves through the damage of death, piloting the deceased from one state of existence to another and escorting one another through the transitional phase of the ritual.

Aggregation

The third and final phase of a ritual, aggregation, reestablishes a new equilibrium in the social group. Separation must be completed and the transitory phase brought to an end, since only then can the survivors of a polis reunite with each other. The deceased needs to be established in the realm of the dead, the underworld, or afterlife for the Archaic Greeks. The living need to reaffiliate themselves as a functioning social entity, a polis, that has successfully coped and overcome death's disruption. Two sets of symbolic behaviors comprise this phase of the ritual: burying and celebrating. The suasive activity, in turn, is again accomplished by juxtaposing oppositional elements of the behaviors.

Burial

Earlier in this chapter the various interment apparatus — the size of the pyre, the quality of the receptacle for the remains, and the various sorts of grave goods — were detailed. The process of burial contains a host of behaviors whose function is to convince the living that their polis is restored and that they are rejoined to the deceased. Much as outward symbols of status indicate one's rank and position in a living community, the relative status of the deceased continues at burial. The more wealth and power one commanded in life, the more symbols of wealth and power are bestowed on the deceased at burial. A more elaborate pyre or a more costly urn preserves in death what the individual had attained in life. Communal rupture is lessened by sustaining the accouterments of status; the more prominent the deceased, the greater the scale of display and the more the social self of the deceased is recreated for the survivors in the polis.

That no set of oppositional elements exists in the symbolic behaviors of interment display should occasion no surprise. The rhetorical message is that nothing has changed. The living, through the means and degree of display, validate instead of argue for the relative prominence of the deceased. Symbolic behaviors surrounding the placement of grave goods are a much different matter.

At the graveside, the mourners of the polis communicated with the earth not for the sake of the deceased but for the continuation of their community. "By burying the dead in the earth and making offerings of fruit, grain, and flowers it was believed that the earth could be repaid for the gift of life, since earth was nurse and mother of all things, and so fertility could be promoted."[23] Other grave goods were expressions of care and concern for the dead person. Food, clothing, adornments, and weapons were the polis's way of sharing its resources for the welfare of the deceased in his or her future spiritual life.

Two other behaviors at the graveside merit attention, namely, the outstretching of the right arm and the adding of a lock of one's own hair to the grave offerings.

Alexiou recreates the scene from archaeological evidence:

Offerings were never made in silence. The vase-paintings show the mourners approaching with their gifts: there were not usually more than two, one always a woman and on foot, sometimes followed by a man who enters from the right on horseback or on foot, leading his horse. The woman then lays her offerings on the tomb and begins her supplication, either kneeling down in earnest prayer with her right arm outstretched, or standing with the right arm in the same position and the left tearing her loosened hair.[24]

Were one to assume the use of right-handed gesturing here as well as in the laying out ceremony was a stylized signal of greeting or farewell one would probably be in error. Symbolic behaviors, after all, are multivocalic and the gesture might have been used for leave-taking. Quite a number of other readings are equally possible, however. Anthropologists have observed "handedness" in the rituals of many primitive cultures and their conclusions are most helpful in interpreting the rhetoric of this symbolic behavior.

In his book *Death and the Right Hand*, Robert Hertz reviews a mass of ethnographic literature and places the concept of "handedness" for primitive societies in the opposition between the sacred and the profane. Within this polarity right-handedness is used to express ideas of physical strength and dexterity, intellectual rectitude and good judgment, uprightness and moral integrity, good fortune and beauty, and juridical norm; while the word "left" evokes most of the ideas contrary to these.[25]

For the pre-Classical Greeks the funeral ceremony was a religious activity and, as such, the supernatural needed to be addressed within the ritual. The formal right-handed gestures used by the Greek mourners reflected their religious beliefs. Hertz explains the substance of the communicative behavior:

> The hands are used only incidentally for the expression of ideas: they are primarily instruments with which man acts on the beings and things that surround him. It is in the diverse fields of human activity that we must observe the hands at work. In worship man seeks above all to communicate with sacred powers, in order to maintain and increase them, and to draw to himself the benefits of their action. Only the right hand is fit for these beneficial relations, since it participates in the nature of the things and beings on which the rites are to act. The gods are on our right, so we turn towards the right to pray. A holy place must be entered right foot first. Sacred offerings are presented to the gods with the right hand. It is the right hand that receives favours from heaven and which transmits them in the benediction.[26]

For the members of the polis the right-handed gesture can be viewed as a rhetorical act of invoking blessings on the deceased, identifying oneself as holding shared religious values with others in the community, and requesting divine favor from the spirit of the deceased.

In both the account of Patroklos' funeral and in that of the ordinary citizen of a polis, mourners at the graveside cut a lock of their hair and added it as an offering along with the other grave goods. The precise meaning of this behavior, more than likely, can never be known. Parallel evidence from anthropologists' studies,[27] however, suggest a range of possibilities. For many primitive cultures one's hair was believed to be the location of an external soul[28] or that one's strength and power resided therein.[29] Arnold Van Gennep's explanation is more directly applicable to the use of such behavior at a burial site. "In reality, what is called 'the sacrifice of the hair' includes two distinct operations: cutting the hair, and dedicating, consecrating, or sacrificing it. To cut the hair is to separate oneself from the previous world; to dedicate the hair is to bind oneself to the sacred world and more particularly to a deity or a spirit with whom kinship is in this way established."[30]

Rhetorically, cutting a lock of hair and placing it in the grave can be understood as a message of collective solidarity. All mourners in the polis engaged in the same action and, thus, by doing so reaffirmed the cohesion of their beliefs. Note also that the collective, dedicatory message is directed at the deceased. The symbolic behavior, therefore, visually links the living community with the dead person or, more accurately, the dead person's spirit. In other words, the message is one of aggregation—the living with each other and the living with the soul of the deceased.

Again, the absence of oppositional elements within the performance of the "offering of hair" behavior should occasion little surprise. At this phase of the ritual separation and marginalization are completed for all practical purposes. Little need remains to produce a "choose life or choose death" situation. The internal rhythm and impetus of the ritual itself reaches a stage, at burial, where transformation is assumed by the collective. The community, however, has realigned and reincorporated itself and this reincorporation has included the deceased in the new spiritual state. With burial completed, the polis celebrated.

Celebrating

A common feature of most rituals is a meal, a feast, or a banquet typically positioned at or near the end of the ceremony. Highly appropriate as a collective act of aggregation, the act of sharing a meal is a particular type of union. "The rite of eating and drinking together . . . is clearly a rite of incorporation, of physical union, and has been called a sacrament of communion."[31] Psychologically, an extended surfeit of any single emotion becomes debilitating for an individual. Just as prolonged sadness or grief in an individual can incapacitate and damage, the same is true for a collectivity, a polis. Participating in a full-scale funeral ceremony, of necessity, had to be an emotionally exhausting experience for the Greeks. Communal sorrow requires communal joy, not as a distraction but as an opposition. Hugh Duncan expresses the same idea:

> In eating, drinking, dancing, and singing together at communal feasts, individuals strengthen their social bonds. There is an intense feeling of unity, as individuals lose themselves in joyful celebration. Under the stimulus of food, drink, song, dance, play and all the arts of merriment, our love and devotion to each other mounts as we rejoice in our fellowship. For if the community is sustained in the solemn concourses of tragic drama, and the rites of sacred ceremony, it is also refreshed in the joy of feasting together in laughter and fun.[32]

Sharing a meal with others elevates the act of self nourishment to that of a social activity. Sharing a meal with others as part of a ritual shifts the action to that of a symbolic behavior fraught with meaning. The very sustenance of life can be viewed, touched, smelled, and tasted—sensed and appreciated—communally. The feasting members of a pre-Classical Greek polis could only have reinforced, for themselves, the value and importance of life and living.[33]

The pattern of the funeral ceremony just described retained its essential characteristics in the Classical Era for many centuries. In the fifth century B.C., however, a significant addition, a highly rhetorical addition, was made in Athens.

NOTES

1. John A. Scott, *Homer and His Influence* (New York: Cooper Square Publishers, Inc., 1963), 101. In subsequent chapters Scott details Homer's impact on Rome, the Renaissance, and England.
2. Scott, *Homer* 96.
3. *The Iliad of Homer*, trans. Richard Lattimore (Chicago: University of Chicago Press, 1951). All references to the *Iliad* are to this edition. By far, the best single source for funeral ceremonies in Ancient Greece is Donna C. Kurtz and John Boardman, *Greek Burial Customs* (Ithaca, NY: Cornell University Press, 1971). Their de-

scriptions of archaeological evidence extends from the Bronze Age to Hellenistic Greece.

4. Embalming as a method of preserving the corpse was unknown to the Greeks. The laying out ceremony can also be read in the *Odyssey* 24.63–6. For laments see *Odyssey*, 24.45–64.

5. Cf. Ian Morris, *Burial and Ancient Society: The Rise of the Greek City State* (New York: Cambridge University Press, 1987), p. 46 observes that "Patroklos' funeral also included lavish sacrifices on the pyre (*Iliad* 23.266–83), which was itself huge (23.164–5). Pyres were also graded in size, with energy expenditure determined by status. It took nine days to collect the wood for Hector's pyre (*Iliad* 24.784), while a single day sufficed to gather the corpses of the masses slaughtered in *Iliad* books 2–7, to collect the fuel, and to complete the cremation (*Iliad* 7.417–32)."

6. For the relationship between status and the size of the burial mound see Morris, *Burial*, 46; Kurtz and Boardman, *Greek Burial*, 12.

7. Cf. *Odyssey* 24.85–82. Also Roger Dunkle, "Nestor, Odysseus, and The *Metis–Bia Antithesis*: The Funeral Games, *Iliad* 23," *Classical World* 81 (September–October, 1987): 1–22.

8. Here and elsewhere I am greatly indebted to Margaret Alexiou, *The Ritual Lament in Greek Tradition* (London: Cambridge University Press, 1974). Her close textual analysis is invaluable. See also Kurtz and Boardman, *Greek Burial*, ch. 7.

9. Alexiou, *Ritual Lament*, 5.

10. Alexiou, *Ritual Lament*, 6.

11. Alexiou, *Ritual Lament*, 11. Kurtz and Boardman, *Greek Burial*, 202 discuss these activities in these words:

> There must have been, it seems, some danger that an ordinary Greek funeral might degenerate into a display of money and noise: wailing at the bier, the carrying out and burial; a richly dressed bier and body; splendid offerings; guests to be entertained after the burial; a tomb monument which would do as much honour to the survivors as to the deceased. While most other religious activities in public were conducted by professional priests, this was one conducted by private persons—the next of kin. It is not surprising, therefore, that nearly all the evidence we have about legislation for burials is concerned with limiting expense, noise and the period of mourning.

12. For the use of music at funerals, Alexiou, *Ritual Lament*, ch. 1, n. 28.

13. Alexiou, *Ritual Lament*, 7.
14. *Lyra Graeca*, trans. J. M. Edmonds (Cambridge, MA: Harvard University Press, 1958), 2.291.
15. Morris, *Burial*, 3. Also M. I. Finley, *The Legacy of Greece* (Oxford: Oxford University Press), 22–36.
16. Aristotle, *Politics*, 1.2.
17. Morris, *Burial*, 5.
18. Arnold van Gennep, *The Rites of Passage*, trans. Monika B. Vizedom and Gabrielle L. Caffee (Chicago: The University of Chicago Press, 1960); Robert Hertz, *Death and the Right Hand*, trans. Rodney and Claudia Needham (Glencoe, IL: The Free Press, 1960). Also Morris, *Burial*, 30 although I differ somewhat with his understanding of the phases.
19. Alexiou develops this consequence in great detail. See 20ff.
20. Morris, *Burial*, 51.
21. Alexiou, *Ritual Lament*, 7.
22. van Gennep, *Rites*, 186: "For example, carrying and being carried is one of the practices which is found more or less universally in the various ceremonies through which a person passes in the course of a lifetime. The subject of the ceremony must not touch the ground for a specific length of time. He is carried in someone's arms or in a litter, placed on a horse, an ox, or in a carriage; he is placed on a mat which is movable or fastened, on a scaffold or an elevated seat, or on a throne. This rite is basically different from that of straddling something or being transported over something, although the two are sometimes combined. The idea is that the person should be raised above or lifted onto something." What I have here labeled "marginalization" is sometimes called "liminality" by other writers. For example, Victor Turner in *The Ritual Process: Structure and Anti-Structure* (Chicago: Aldine Publishing Co., 1969), 94 describes the phase in this way:

> The attributes of liminality or of liminal personae ("threshold people") are necessarily ambiguous, since this condition and these persons elude or slip through the network of classifications that normally locate states and positions in cultural space. Liminal entities are neither here nor there; they are betwixt and between the positions assigned and arrayed by law, custom, convention, and ceremonial. As such, their ambiguous and indeterminate attributes are expressed by a rich variety of symbols in the many societies that ritualize social and cultural transitions. Thus, luminality is frequently likened to death, to being in the womb, to invisibility, to darkness, to bisexuality, to the wilderness, and to an eclipse of the sun or moon.

Turner develops this description in his essay, "Liminality and the Performative Genres," in *Rite, Drama, Festival, Spectacle: Rehearsals Toward a Theory of Cultural Performance*, ed. John J. Mac-Aloon, 19–41 (Philadelphia: Institute for the Study of Human Sciences, 1984).

23. Alexiou, *Ritual Lament*, 9.
24. Alexiou, *Ritual Lament*, 8.
25. Hertz, *Death*, 99.
26. Hertz, *Death*, 104.
27. Earnest Crawley, *The Mystic Rose: A Study of Primitive Thought in its Bearing on Marriage* (New York: Boni and Liveright, 1927), 1.289, 336; 2.117. Also James George Frazer, *The Golden Bough* (New York: The MacMillan Co., 1922).
28. Frazer, *Golden Bough*, 670.
29. Frazer, *Golden Bough*, 680.
30. van Gennep, *Rites*, 166.
31. van Gennep, *Rites*, 29.
32. Hugh Dalziel Duncan, *Symbols in Society* (New York: Oxford University Press, 1968), 181.
33. One might wonder at the apparent omission of any discussion of monuments and tombstones. Since these were erected by a family and not the community, it seemed consistent to omit them. An interested reader might consult J. W. Day "Rituals in Stone: Early Greek Epigrams and Monuments," *The Journal of Hellenic Studies* 109 (1989):16–28. Also Philippe Aries, *Western Attitudes Toward Death: From the Middle Ages to the Present*, trans. Patricia M. Ranum (Baltimore: The Johns Hopkins Press, 1974). Aries believes tombs represent "the survivor's unwillingness to accept the departure of their loved one" (70).

Chapter Four

The Athenian State Funeral Ceremony

The Classical Greek funeral ceremony did not remain unchanged and unaffected by cultural shifts. The Greece of the
Archaic Period (750 B.C.–500 B.C.) was different in many significant ways from the Greece of the Classical Era (500 B.C.–332
B.C.). The most fundamental change and the one with the most
direct impact on the form and substance of the funeral ritual
was the political shift to a democratic form of government in
the polis of Athens. In other city-states where monarchies, ti-
mocracies, plutocracies, and oligarchies continued more or less
unchanged, the ritual did not change in any appreciable way.
From Athens, however, the greatest quantity of literary evidence about their funeral ceremonies remains and, as a consequence, this chapter will focus on the ritual used there. Athens
was atypical, if not actually unique, and the relationships between Athenian democracy and Athenian rituals of consolation
can be reconstructed and reviewed as a direct consequence of
the extant literary evidence and the sizable body of scholarship
about this evidence.

The rise of democratic institutions in Athens is familiar
grist for the mills of many historians. The multiple and multifaceted impacts of the Ionian philosophers; pre-Classical colo-
nization; the "reforms" of Draco, Cleisthenes, and Solon; the
Dorian migration; the broadening of the class base for military
service; the growth of slavery; the development of international
commerce; the decline of religious belief; and, most certainly,
the defeat of the Persians (490 B.C.–479 B.C.) all played a part
in the change.[1] None of these factors should be minimized; each
definitely altered the political, social, and cultural milieu of
Athens. One other historical force, a force rarely connected to
change in the Greek funeral ceremony, was the teaching of the
Sophists. As Hermann Bergston says, "The teachings of the
Sophists were a decisive factor in moulding the character of the

new Hellenic personality. They actually brought about a revo-
lution in Greek culture, their effects perceptible in every sphere
of life, and not least in politics."[2] Who they were and what they
taught is the subject of the first section in this chapter.

The Early Sophists

In his book *Sophists, Socratics, and Cynics*, H. D. Rankin
characterizes the sophists as a profession.

> They were a profession, but not a homogeneous one. Their
> main points in common were that they were paid for their
> teaching and that they based their teaching upon devel-
> oped uses of language for imparting skill in argument and
> persuasion. Whether an individual Sophist's claim was to
> teach *arete* (virtue) or merely some argumentative tech-
> nique or way of arranging language in the most impres-
> sive or convincing style, his concern was with the human
> realm and the association of man with man in the com-
> petitive life of Greek society.[3]

For the Sophists a mastery of rhetoric was the key to success in politics. Teaching in an oral mode to audiences powerfully influenced by the spoken word, they presented exhibition
speeches or conducted seminars in the art of making lengthy,
persuasive speeches. Truth as an end of an argument was of
less concern than winning a case in the courts of successfully
urging a proposal in the legislature. Aristotle and Plato cen-
sured both their methods of teaching, which challenged the
aristocratic tutorial method of earlier centuries, and their disregard for truth, as defined by religion and the aristocracy. The
most prominent features of their teaching—arguments based
on probabilities (*eikota*)[4] and custom (*nomos*)[5] would seem most
likely to influence the funeral ceremony. Such was not the case.
Not until literary forms of consolation emerged in the first century B.C. (see chapter 6) did Sophistic argumentation become
significant.

The Sophists, however, also taught ways to make one's style
charming, forceful, and lively through the use of poetic devices
and word choice.[6] The training in rhetorical style offered by the
Sophists is quite evident in the extant state funeral speeches.

A considerable tension arises when one rejects any notion of permanent moral values, as did the Sophists, yet confronts a rhetorical situation calling for consolation. Death, after all, is a natural law, not a matter of convention or custom. The fact and inevitability of death cannot be changed or denied by *nomos*-based rhetorical discourse. A funeral ceremony, even the unusual type used at Athens, is a custom and one incredibly resistant to revision. For the Archaic Greeks, as was explained in chapter 3, the funeral ritual contained much that was based in unquestioned religious beliefs, *physis*, or nature, as divine law. In the fifth century, however, conditions were right for making a number of changes in the Athenian ritual of consolation. The practice could well have been significantly altered, but it was not.

Athenian Consolatory Practice

Although the passage is somewhat lengthy, Thucydides' description reveals much about the symbolic behavior used in the Athenian funeral ceremony.

In the course of the same winter the Athenians, following the custom of their fathers, celebrated at the public expense the funeral rites of the first who had fallen in this war. The ceremony is as follows. The bones of the departed lie in state for the space of three days in a tent erected for that purpose, and each one brings to his own dead any offering he desires. On the day of the funeral coffins of cypress wood are borne on wagons, one for each tribe, and the bones of each are in the coffin of his tribe. One empty bier, covered with a pall, is carried in the procession for the missing whose bodies could not be found for burial. Any one who wishes, whether citizen or stranger, may take part in the funeral procession, and the women who are related to the deceased are present at the burial and make lamentation. The coffins are laid in the public sepulchre, which is situated in the most beautiful suburb of the city; there they always bury those fallen in war, except indeed those who fell at Marathon; for their valor the Athenians judged to be preeminent and they buried them on the spot where they fell. But when the remains have been laid away in the earth, a man chosen by the state, who is regarded as best endowed with wisdom and is foremost in public esteem, delivers over them an appropriate eulogy. After this the people depart. In this manner they bury; and throughout the war, whenever occasion arose, they observed this custom.[7]

A number of other action and object languages were employed in this elaborate funeral ceremony. If the dead soldiers left orphans in the polis, the state took responsibility for raising and educating them. Survivors unable to care for themselves were made wards of the state and received their meals at public expense. All costs for the funeral, the monument on which were inscribed the names of the dead, and the cost of a verse epigram added to the monument were paid for by the State. Then, as further recognition of valor on the battlefields, athletic contests, races, and festivals were conducted annually at the burial site.[8]

Symbolic Behaviors

This abundance of symbolic behaviors functions rhetorically to console by a wholesale redefinition of death along with its personal and social consequences of loss. Again, elements of the symbolic behaviors are set in opposition so that audience members are urged to accept one pole of the opposing terms thereby creating a context in which consolation could happen. Since the intensity of the symbolic behaviors in the ceremony can be interpreted as a direct and directed effort to restore social cohesion after losing family members in war, a closer analysis of the symbolic behaviors is clearly warranted.

How distant in time from the State ceremony an actual soldier's death took place is uncertain. Wars were typically waged after the crops were planted in the spring. Conceivably, then, a soldier could have been killed six to nine months before the State ceremony, and private funeral services already completed. By conducting the state ceremony in the winter months private rituals were set in opposition to a public ritual. Individual loss would be redefined as a public loss. Personal grief would be reset as the collective grief of the polis since the cause of each death was identical—death by battle in the service of the state.

In the older custom a single day for viewing the body was the norm. The Athenian service provided for a two day viewing period but, again, all the survivors conduct their laments and offerings in concert with and in sight of other community members.[9] As a political group Athens consisted of ten tribes, or demes. At a private funeral, most probably, only members of one's deme would participate, but the State funeral would bring together a wider, more extended social group. Participants in the State ritual were placed in a social context and a rhetorical situation wherein the public sharing of their sorrow would invite a lessening of the intense, interior psychological distress of loss.

The scale of a private ceremony was set in opposition to the scale of the State ritual. In the private funeral rite the procession would be small relative to the large movement at the state ceremony. A single dead person would be carried to the burial site, typically a site outside the city. Athenian processions carried multiple remains to a site within the city.[10] For private funerals the remains were placed in clay urns; the State funeral offered coffins of cypress, a wood prized for its impermeability and sufficiently scarce that a fine of three years salary was levied on any private citizen found guilty of cutting or burning cypress.[11] To die for the polis brought rewards inaccessible to an ordinary citizen's family.

To be denied burial for the Greeks was a sacrilege. How much more painful, then, for survivors not to have the physical remains for a burial ceremony. Battles at sea and wars in foreign lands had to create occasions when bodies were lost or unable to be recovered. No evidence exists to indicate that private ceremonies were held without the actual physical remains—the body was needed. Not so for the State service; those missing in action were clearly recognized by deployment of the empty coffin. Athens honored its valorous warriors whether present or absent.

Not least among the many consequences of death on the survivors is the uncertainty, often economic, of the future. The state funeral sets this uncertainty against a full faith guarantee of certainty by providing for those survivors unable to subsist without such aid. Even in death a deceased citizen soldier, through the aegis of the State, provides for his family as if he were still alive. Sacrifice of oneself for the State benefits the living.

Rhetorically, a warrior's death is differentiated from an ordinary death. The former is accorded symbols, actions, and as a subsequent section will describe, words of laudation, immortality, and status; death from causes other than battle remains a matter of no concern from the state. Death in the State ceremony is denoted as the highest achievement a mortal man can attain. In its rhetorical construction such a death and its positive consequences becomes desirable, not something horrific. A warrior's death is an occasion to celebrate but not to disregard, to commemorate but not to simply accept.

Even in selecting the orator to deliver the funeral oration an element of opposition in the symbolic behavior is present. Not just anyone is selected for what is considered an honor. Not a relative, not a socially prominent member of one's tribe, but, as Thucydides says, "a man chosen by the state, who is regarded as best endowed with wisdom and is foremost in public esteem," is selected to present the eulogy. The highest social status of a living individual thereby was conferred on the collective deaths of the honorees.

One other feature deserves mention, not because it contains oppositional elements, but because, in itself, it removes existing oppositions. In the State funeral ceremony all who died are buried physically intermingled and in a common, albeit quite luxurious, burial ground. Prior social differences— rich/poor, aristocratic/common, urban/rural, brave/cowardly, strong/weak, etc.—are symbolically removed and made irrelevant. All, in death, are equal and equally valued in the state ceremony.

An integral part of the Athenian consolatory ritual was the funeral oration, a genre often studied[12] and a form of public address continuously used even to the present day. Classical rhetorical theorists did include the genre in their discussions of persuasion[13] but in a strict historic sense the practice of eulogy precedes the theorizing. Consequently, an analysis of the extant speeches themselves will yield the basis for much of the theorizing.

The Athenian Funeral Oration

Loraux begins her treatise on the subject with these ideas:

> In the catalogue of Athenian inventions the funeral oration may not be in the forefront, but it has an honorable place: after the enumeration of the canonical benefits of the democratic city, but in the first rank of Athenian idiomatic forms. Outdistanced by the great inventions of civilization, which were of mythical origin and of universal import, and which testify that, in the race for the prize of philanthropia, the Athenians came first, the *epitaphios logos* comes into its own on the glorious field of arete, where it has no rival. To prove that "among the Greeks only the Athenians know how to honor valor," one has only to declare, with Demosthenes, that "they alone in the world deliver funeral orations for citizens who have died for their country."[14]

Indeed, were one totally unacquainted with a Greek funeral oration and knew only the particulars of the action and object languages of the symbolic behaviors in the ritual one would expect to find a type of discourse that privileges and valorizes those who died in battle. The rhetorical situation itself demands that the dead be praised but much more is also determined by the situation. The living, too, must be addressed, shared values voiced and reinforced, loss recontextualized, and consolation sought. Insofar as such an oration becomes a fixture in the funeral ceremony it rapidly becomes a less flexible form of address. That is, audience expectations increasingly constrain what a speaker can or cannot do and can or cannot say. As an integral part of a ritual, the speech itself becomes, or can tend to become, rigid in form and substance. The way it was done in the past controls, to a great extent, what can be done on subsequent occasions.

Six funeral orations and several fragments are extant[15] although all but one of the orations are problematic. Pericles delivered the State funeral address in 431 B.C., but we have only the text written by Thucydides, the historian. Lysias wrote an oration (ca. 392 B.C.) but he was a foreigner and would not have been allowed to deliver it. Too, we have fragments of a funeral oration in the extant works of Gorgias of Leontini (ca. 426 B.C.) but he also was not an Athenian. Plato's *Menexenus* (ca. 386 B.C.) contains a fictive and ironic funeral address which was not delivered. Demosthenes was credited with writing a State funeral speech (ca. 338 B.C.), but it was later determined to be spurious. Only one speech, that of Hyperides (ca. 322 B.C.) represents an authentic, actually delivered funeral oration. One can safely claim that the State funeral oration was not only an institution but also a literary form and, as Poulakos has recently observed, if read across time, an historic record.[16]

When the need for such State discourse arose already existing literary forms, the lament, the encomium, and the victory ode, served as situationally constraining genres. George Thomson, for example, indicates several key differences among these preexisting literary forms, differences that are significant. He observes: "The funeral oration was related to the lament, from which it differed in being spoken, not sung. It was also related to the encomium which was a speech in praise of the living; and the encomium was related to the victory ode from which it differed in being spoken, not sung, and addressed to a man, not a god."[17] Why are these differences important?

Freed from the conventions of meter the funeral oration would have greater latitude in stylistic, rather than stylized, expression. Yet, the situational demand for discourse that recognized and shared sorrow and grief would remain. To feature lamentation as the predominate motif in a State funeral oration, however, would risk counterproductive and undesirable effects not least of which would be the arousal of intense and debilitating emotions along with the possibility of questioning deaths in State instigated wars. Laments, as such, are minimized in the extant orations and, when they are included the lament is subsumed in the second main section of the oration, the consolation.[18]

An encomium, on the other hand, offered a ready-made structure and tradition for the funeral oration. To praise a living person, as Isocrates does in his *Evagoras*, an orator had received a set of topics: noble birth, upbringing, wealth, health, physical and mental excellences, honors, virtues, etc.[19] For the situational needs of a State funeral oration, then, an orator, for the most part, could simply adapt the familiar and already recognizable topics used to praise a person in crafting the section of the speech praising the polis itself.

Poetic celebrations of victory, a third precursor of the funeral orations, can be read in the works of Simonides, Baccylides, and Pindar and this genre of discourse sets many of the themes that recur in the State funeral address. Victory odes were hymns of praise celebrating the athletic accomplishments of the sons of aristocrats. Success, achievement, and victory were lauded and the living, human world was joined to that of the gods. Faced with the necessity of praising those fallen in battle and the concomitant need to praise the living, the victory ode format proved to be a valuable resource as well as a culturally controlling mechanism. For example, the funeral oration could rhetorically construct the State as not a mere political institution but a supernatural force with godlike powers. Too, the same virtues extolled in a victorious athlete—courage, endurance, bravery, daring, valor, stamina, etc.—could be adapted as descriptors for those who died in battle. To an audience accustomed to hearing a living individual praised for displaying such virtues, the same audience, hearing their dead relatives depicted as possessing the same qualities, would most probably accept the implied conclusion that death in battle is praiseworthy and cause for celebration not lamentation.

An overriding motif of praise was the predominant trait of the orations. Detailing this praise Poulakos says:

> In burial speeches, the discourse of glorification assumed the form of an impersonal narrative, a chronological account of Athens' past. Occupying the larger portion of the speech, the narrative unfolded in a linear account of heroic deeds from the earliest origins of Athens to its most recent victories in war, a chronicle of the city's renowned accomplishments. Made up of both real and mythical events, and expressed in the hyperbolic language of praise, these laudatory accounts of past deeds became one of the earliest forms of history in the classical period.[20]

Glorifying Athens' record of success and achievement within the repeated ritual context of the State funeral service produced problems both of form and content. K. R. Walters, for example, catalogs the difficulties in this way:

> Further, the contents of the speeches were remarkably static: traditional themes and *exampla* were recited with little or no change year after year, in speech after speech. Although some originality and variation were permitted, the speakers were constrained to work within very close limits. Indeed, the constant repetition of commonplace themes gives the orations a formulaic, almost liturgical quality. Yet, though less lofty in artistic expression or undistinguished for individual brilliance, these speeches fulfilled an important, indeed vital, social function for the Athenians. However hackneyed its themes may seem, the funeral oration was a true *vox populi*: it promulgated a message that was hardly the personal expression of the orators, but rather the collective voice of the Athenian polity. In sum, the orations were designed not to inform or to innovate, but to articulate in ritual fashion shared community ideals, values, and attitudes.[21]

Before analyzing the means of praise and the thematic approaches to discursive consolation in the State funeral orations, a significant question needs to be addressed. How does inflexible, formulaic praise function rhetorically to serve consolatory purposes? In other words, is it not paradoxical that in extolling, often with hyperbole, the great glory of the state the intensity of grief and loss would be exacerbated and increased? The dead have not only lost their lives but also lost any further opportunity to share in and partake of the many excellences of the polis. The living, not the dead, win battles, create cultural institutions, engage in virtuous acts, right wrongs, draft laws, and extend the benefits of freedom to others. How, then, does praise console rhetorically?

Depending on a critic's ideology a range of probable answers can be given. For example, one who opposes war, in principle and in practice, might well read the several centuries of Athenian State funeral orations as a "great lie." Athenian aristocrats needed troops for their armies and, to insure a continuing supply of citizen soldiers, the inevitable casualties were institutionally redefined in terms of noble sacrifice, a glorious choice, and a full measure of love for one's country. Those who die in battle become invested, posthumously, with such laudatory virtues as boldness, daring, courage, bravery, nobility, intelligence, and fortitude. Culturally, Athens loved both peace and victory, an inconsistency that ultimately proved fatal for the polis.[22] However, a "great lie" interpretation relies more on political explanation than on rhetorical function. Also, an explanation based on a privileged class engaged in exploitation fails to account for the absence of any resistance to military service. Ultimately, such a reading gives more power to words than is warranted.

Another answer to the question, how does praise rhetorically console, might minimize the funeral oration thereby placing it in the broader context of the entire ceremony. Within a three day ceremony filled with action and object languages the address of a single individual can be seen as a very small part. Such an interpretation does not take into account the Athenian love of language, particularly, the language of display. Oratory for the Athenians was an art form and any effort to reduce its social importance would be an unfortunate error.

Praise in the service of consolation, I maintain, does work because it supplies an acceptable, and needed, reply to the constellation of questions survivors have when a loved one dies suddenly from nonnatural causes. Being killed in a military action is such a death. In these cases survivors experience sorrow and grief but the circumstances create a special climate of questioning, inquiry in search of reasons capable of modifying grief or, at best, offering explanations as to why the death was necessary and whether the death had any meaning. The quality of one's sudden death can be consoling to survivors by describing the degree of altruism involved in the death. To illustrate in more contemporary terms, a person killed by lightning while bicycling and a person drowned while attempting to save a child are both dead but the qualitative circumstances of the latter's death can be a basis for consoling survivors. In the ostensible act of praising the altruistic motive, a socially revered and timeless quality is attached to the deceased.

Although the dead cannot be restored to life the deceased can be invested, through publicly addressed language, with a kind of symbolic immortality. Assuming that one freely chooses, that is actively wills oneself, to engage in a military battle, one also voluntarily chooses to accept the consequences one of which can be death. However, the primary intent is not to die; the volitional goal is to win the military engagement. A rhetorician can offer to the living, in the act of praising the war dead, reasons why an individual risked death and place the positive consequences of the death into a broad societal perspective of exemplary behavior. For the living, considerable comfort can be taken in being told (and believing) that the deceased died a meaningful death for altruistic reasons. If life is indeed precious, then whatever one willfully gives one's life for, is, or can be shown to be, even more precious. A greater good supersedes a great loss.

Yet another intrinsic feature of the State funeral oration functions rhetorically to console survivors, a feature noted and regularly dismissed or denigrated by critics. Many readers label the substance of the orations as static, repetitious, and formulaic. Adjudged against literary standards these are valid and accurate labels but a closer inspection of the general structure, the common lines of development, and the language itself indicates that liturgical not literary standards are more appropriate bases for assessment.

Structure

Later critics and theorists codified the essential organizational pattern used by the funeral orators. Menander and Pseudo-Dionysius, for example, wrote manuals that offer prescriptive outlines for one to follow in presenting such a speech.[23] One must note, as many scholars have, that these manuals were composed five centuries after the practice of State funeral oratory originated and that the manual writers were directing their efforts toward orators at private rather than public funerals.[24] As a consequence the manuals reflect structural differences and lines of development simply not used and not found in the six extant funeral orations. "Both rhetoricians, for example, discuss the topics of birth (genesis), nature (physis), and upbringing (agage), which are not found in the extant funeral orations."[25] Also, the theorists differ about the need to include a lament in a State funeral speech. Differences and variations notwithstanding, an acceptable overview of the structural pattern can be acquired by viewing Menander's prescriptions (see Table 4.1) and, at the same time, noting both problems and cautions.

TABLE 4.1
MENANDER'S OUTLINE OF GENERAL HEADINGS

   I. Introductory comments
  II. Praise (*epainos*) of the polis and those being buried
 III. Lament (*threnos*)
      (N. B. only Lysias' speech has a lament. Such a heading would be
      necessary at a private funeral and, perhaps, counterproductive at
      a public ceremony.)
  IV. Consolation (*paramythia*)
   V. Conclusion

Within each of the general headings, sets of more or less standard topics, headings that served as lines of development for an orator, formed an essential part of the traditional rubric.[26] These lines of development are displayed in Table 4.2. When developing the standard topic, "Praise of the Dead" orators tended to use commonplaces, short sections amplifying in stylized language a single theme.[27]

This structured list, representing as it does the architecture of the Athenian funeral oration reveals much about the limited arena in which an orator was expected to perform and, at the same time, the limitless power of the structure to alter the perceptions of the participants. Deviations or omissions from the formula were apparently permitted but an orator usually told his audience what he was deviating from or about to omit. Certainly, even in the constrictive structure of the funeral oration the orator could incorporate some freshness and originality via his style of presentation or the relative emphasis and dilation placed on one or another of the expected, and thereby, required topics or general headings. With one's invention and arrangement already determined by the situation only the oratorical arts of memory, delivery, and style remain.

However, within the structure itself several elements, strategically placed in opposition, serve to elicit consolation. Both the living and the dead are featured. The dead are praised, di-

TABLE 4.2
STANDARD TOPICS FOR THE GENERAL HEADINGS

I. Introductory Comments
  1. Approve the tradition
  2. Inadequacy of suitable praise
  3. Inadequate time to prepare
  4. Special excellences of the dead
II. Praise of the Polis and Those Being Buried
  1. Noble beginnings of the ancestors
  2. Glorious deeds of the ancestors
  3. Benefits accruing from the fatherland
    a. politics
    b. customs
    c. practices
    d. education
    e. nourishment both physical and spiritual
  4. Praise of the dead
III. Consolation
  1. Good fortune of the dead and the living
  2. Bad fortune
  3. Exhortation
IV. Conclusion
  1. Tradition is satisfied
  2. The speech is completed
  3. A lament
  4. A consolatory commonplace
  5. An admonition to depart

rectly, for giving their lives for the polis. The living are praised, indirectly, for their role as citizens of Athens. But, note, the living, in the intrinsic structure of the oration, are celebrated as the inheritors and, by extension, those who can continue the many glorious excellences and achievements that characterize the past. The living, not the dead, can continue to enjoy the benefits of living in their country. Sorrow, grief, and loss are minimized; death is a product of good or bad luck, a force over which no one has control. Joy, pride, and superiority are maximized; life as an Athenian is the best of all possible worlds, and, it is for the living to continue increasing the glory and grandeur of the city-state for which one's relatives died. In other words, the rhetoric of the form itself insures that the warriors' deaths will be redefined as meaningful, not meaningless; important, not inconsequential; momentous, not negligible; and significant, not trivial. Personal loss becomes a cause for celebration, not grief, when the loss happened in the service of one's country. Since the State is paramount in all respects it is almost a civic duty, in terms of the oratorical structure, to participate in the ongoing glory of Athens and, thereby, stop grief and be consoled.

Even at the lexical level the auditors were offered a choice between opposites. Popular word-antitheses abound: "common vs. special," a construction appearing no less than forty times in the texts, according to Theodore Burgess, that stresses the unique excellence of the war dead.[28] Funeral orators regularly juxtaposed "words vs. deeds," "justice vs. injustice," "the few vs. the many," "bravery vs. cowardice," etc. In each instance one of the paired concepts is clearly preferable and, by voicing the antithetical term, the desirable term becomes even more desirable, valued, or distinctly praiseworthy. Structurally, an antithesis closely resembles the antiphonal mode of expression. Both tend to contain a part that asserts and a part that answers, reflects, or extends. In the early Greek laments, the antiphonal mode required two principal actors—a leader and respondent(s) or a leader and a chorus. In the funeral oration the orator is simultaneously the leader of the community and also a member, the speaker and, by virtue of antiphonal language, the chorus. Both the excessive use of antithesis and the quasi-antiphonal structure of the funeral oration (praise vs. consolation) strongly suggest an underlying liturgical dimension in the Athenian epitaph.

Liturgical Constraints

For contemporary readers, no doubt, the concept of liturgy is associated with church services and public worship. More generally the term can be taken to mean "a system or series of ceremonial or ritualistic actions done according to a prescribed arrangement."[29] Most traditional weddings, for example, are conducted according to a set of preexisting procedures. More closely related to gaining an increased understanding of the

Athenian funeral oration, however, is the original use of the term. Theodore Jennings explains:

> The term liturgy is derived from the Greek *leitourgia*, which refers to an act or work (*ergon*) performed by or for the people (*laitos*). In the Greek city-states the term often had the technical political sense of referring to the obligation placed upon wealthy citizens to undertake tasks relating to the common good (building a monument, outfitting a ship, helping to supply an army). It could also be used in a wider sense to refer to any service that one person performed for another.[30]

The Athenians believed it was the responsibility of the well-to-do to aid and assist the polis in special ways. Isocrates, for instance, uses the liturgical duty as the basis for his essay, *On the Antidosis*. Strictly speaking the Athenians did not call or designate the State funeral ceremony a liturgy yet it meets all the necessary and sufficient conditions for being one. That is, the ceremony was corporate in character, cyclical in its production, coordinative of various experiences, and legitimating of authority.[31]

The very fact that the entire funeral ceremony was public makes the activity corporate in character. No one was excluded from participating in the State-initiated service. Designated representatives of the polis specified when the activity would happen and, more importantly, who would present the oration. In a metaphoric if not an almost real sense, then, the orator functioned in ways analogous to an ordained church official in modern times. But, unlike the analogous official, the State orator was not permitted much, if any, freedom of expression in composing an epitaphic address. The very nature of a liturgical performance preempts and precludes excessive deviation from the formulae.

Since the ceremony itself was conducted annually it meets the test of cyclicity. An annual public event of significance to many citizens would also tend, across time, to calcify adherence to the established rubric. Audiences, accordingly, would come to expect neither more nor less than what took place and in what sequence in previously enacted State funerals. Expectations of replication would also serve to control the structure and substance of a funeral oration. The repeated cycle of the State ceremony also structured time "thereby making it available for conscious experience and intellectual comprehension."[32] The dead, for whom the ceremony was held, no longer existed in humanly perceived, actual time. However, the ceremony viewed as a State liturgy functioned to establish the dead warriors in what might be called spiritual time or corporate memory. While the object and action languages associated with the ceremony contributed to this restructuring of time, the words of the orator, extolling the deeds and the rationale of the deeds (i.e., the polis), functioned to keep the dead alive in the memories of the mourners and the citizens of the polis. Praise, the predominate rhetorical objective of the funeral orations, instantiates the dead warriors into a timeless, living history revived and reified each and every year. Whereas the consolatory passages of an oration offered reasons for accepting loss and ending grief, the trademark laudations of past and present, of former glory and current valor create, rhetorically, a social reality of immortality for the dead soldiers. In a real sense one can say that the rhetorical work of the funeral orators gave the dead a new life and the survivors a sufficient basis for consolation.

The funeral orator, in the act of addressing his fellow citizens and viewed here as the momentary conductor of a liturgical function, also coordinated various experiences of the collective in his speech. As Jennings observes, "The complex mirroring of individual, social, and natural or cosmic bodies gives to ritual its evocative power and rich content. In this way liturgy generates the world of shared human experience."[33] When a Lysias, or a Demosthenes, or an Isocrates repeated in their funeral orations the legendary accounts of defeating the Amazons and Heraclidae, or of recovering the bodies of those who died at Thebes, or when a Plato or Gorgias or Hyperides repeat the stories of the Persian Wars and the battle of Salamis, the accounts create a rhetorical constellation of glory and idealized greatness, heroic and godlike in conduct and accomplishment. Pericles' lofty accounting of the preeminence, distinction, and supremacy of Athens can be read as an effort to coordinate the various lived experiences of the audience through his language. Again, viewing the State oration as an integral part of a liturgy one can understand the need for orators to focus on and repeat the topics best suited to regenerating a world of shared human experience. Granting for the moment that repeating stories, topics, and themes—and repeating them for centuries—most probably did function, rhetorically, to construct something of shared world view among the audiences, the question remains, how would such "coordinating of various experiences" console those grieving over the loss of a kinsman?

Aristotle provides the beginning of the answer. "Noble birth," he defines as, "a heritage of honor from one's ancestors."[34] Taken at face value this definition, for a modern reader, would suggest that only an elite, aristocratic parent could produce offspring of nobility. Not the case for Athenians. Aristotle is clear on this point for he qualifies the definition: "The idea of noble birth refers to excellence of race."[35] Recalling that State funeral orators were expected to dilate the theme of noble birth and, as we have seen repeatedly, they did so, one can see the rhetorical dynamic of suasive consolation taking shape. Recast into enthymematic form the underlying reasoning would be:

All Athenians enjoy noble birth. The dead warriors are Athenians. Those who lost kinsman are Athenians. As Athenians, the dead, because of the valorous circumstances of their deaths, are clearly deserving of the honor bestowed on them by their ancestors.

As honorable Athenians, the dead warriors now become ancestors for future generations of Athenians and, consequently, they not only live in memory they continue to serve an important social function. As Athenians, those who lost kinsmen can be consoled because the dead remain socially and spiritually alive.

Understanding the Athenian term of noble birth not in a biological but in a racial sense, therefore, clarifies the need for a static form in the orations and the resultant suasory dimension. Individuals of the same race might die, but the race itself remains alive, constant, and stable. An oration praising a race cannot change or fluctuate in any significant way.

Viewing the Athenian State funeral ceremony and its inclusion of an oration as a liturgy one final perspective on the rhetorical function of the publicly addressed epitaph can be gained. In the earlier private Greek funeral no person was designated as a leader, manager, or, better yet, an individual who served as a conduit between the physical and spiritual worlds. The Athenian funeral orator did function as a quasi-religious leader helping the survivors adapt to their loss by focusing on the "prelife" of community, not an "afterlife" in our contemporary sense. This distinction seems significant in that it is amenable to a rhetoric of opposition as presented in earlier chapters. In modern times and for many cultures one dies and one's spirit goes to some geographic location on, under, or in the earth. For the Athenian war dead, as a consequence of the rhetorical glorifications, one does not "go to" but instead one "remains" among and alongside those who made Athens the best of all city-states. The orator serves as a secular minister, in a sense, in that consolation is offered to the survivors by way of redirection in addition to redefinition. The fact of physical death is not denied but the psychological experience of loss is redirected to a rhetorically constituted experience of gain. Thus, the Athenian State, speaking through the designated orator-minister, legitimates its authority as the institution for which one dies and within which, in death, one lives.

NOTES

1. See for example Anton Powell, *Athens and Sparta: Constructing Greek Political and Social History from 478 B.C.* (Portland, OR: Areopagitica Press, 1988); Raphael Sealey, *A History of the Greek City States, 700–338 B.C.* (Berkeley: University of California Press, 1976); Michael Grant, *The Rise of the Greeks* (New York: Macmillan Publishing Co., 1987); and Hermann Bergston, *History of Greece: From the Beginnings to the Byzantine Era*, trans. Edmund F. Bloedow (Ottawa: University of Ottawa Press, 1988).

2. Bergston, *History of Greece*, 134.

3. H. D. Rankin, *Sophists, Socratics, and Cynics* (Totowa, NJ: Barnes and Noble Books, 1983), 14. In recent years the Sophists have received increased attention from many scholars. One might profitably consult: W. K. C. Guthrie, *The Sophists* (Cambridge: Cambridge University Press, 1971); G. B. Kerford, *The Sophist Movement* (Cambridge: Cambridge University Press, 1981); *The Older Sophists: A Complete Translation by Several Hands of the*

Fragments in Die Fragmente Der Vorsokratiker Edited by Diels-Kranz With a New Edition of Antiphon and of Euthydemus, ed. Rosamond Kent Sprague (Columbia, SC: University of South Carolina Press, 1972); and John Poulakos, "Rhetoric, the Sophists, and the Possible," *Communication Monographs* 51 (1984):215–26.

4. Guthrie, *The Sophists*, 50.

5. Guthrie, *The Sophists*, 55.

6. Cf. Aristotle, *Rhetoric*, 3.

7. Thucydides, *History of the Peloponnesian War*, trans. Charles Forster Smith (Cambridge, MA: Harvard University Press, 1921–1930), 2.34.1–7. A clarification on the phrase, "The *bones* of the departed lie in state," may be helpful for a reader. Cremation, as practiced by the Greeks and Romans did not and could not produce "ashes" or "cremains" as most contemporary readers would normally assume, given our modern practices and language use. The open-air pyre used in classical times would produce temperatures between 500–800°F. To place this fact in perspective one should know that human skin blisters at 170°F; a burning wood-frame building would reach temperatures from 800–1,200°F; and, our modern crematoria use temperatures in excess of 2,400°F for several hours. Human bones, essentially calcium, do not burn even in our crematoria. What we call "ashes" are pulverized bone particles. For the Athenian State ceremony, then, families would be able to disinter the actual bones of the deceased. For this technical information I am indebted to Michelle Ochs, M.D., University of Iowa Hospitals; Dean Trump, Assistant Fire Chief, Solon Fire Department, Solon, IA; and Jeffrey Roland, President, Wilbert Crematorium and Vault Co., Cedar Rapids, IA.

8. Nicole Loraux, *The Invention of Athens: The Funeral Oration in the Classical City*, trans. Alan Sheridan (Cambridge, MA: Harvard University Press, 1986), 17–28.

9. Larry J. Bennett and Wm. Blake Tyrrell, "Sophocles' *Antigone* and Funeral Oratory," *American Journal of Philology* 111 (1990):444 elaborated some of the more significant changes in this description: "To create a democratic, that is, public funeral, the demos appropriated rites of aristocratic funerals which its legislation had been continually restricting since Solon. The demos displayed the bones for two days, twice that allowed private funerals, under a tent in the agora (Thuc. 2.34). Here families mourned their husbands, sons, and brothers with whatever customs they wished. This concession to familial loss and grief, loosened from normal curbs on public display, contrasts the first two days with the rituals of the third. On the dawning of this day, no longer are

the bones distinguished by the names, identities, and economic and social differences that separated individuals in life. Now they are 'the dead,' an expression virtually synonymous with the city and reified by the organization of the remains in boxes according to the Cleisthenian tribes. Wagons carrying the chests formed a procession more elaborate than any family could mount. While laws denied the family's right to bring outsiders, slaves, strangers, and paid mourners into its funerals, anyone could join in the public ceremony."

10. In the lengthy quotation from Thucydides the phrase, "most beautiful suburb of the city," refers to an area known as the Kerameikos. See Loraux, *Invention*, 19ff.

11. John Perlin, *A Forest Journey: The Role of Wood in the Development of Civilization* (New York: W. W. Norton, 1989), 97. For an exhaustive list of the indestructable and immortal "virtues" of cypress and their classical references, see Loraux, *Invention*, 349 n. 26.

12. A representative sampling would include: K. R. Walters, "Rhetoric as Ritual: The Semiotics of the Attic Funeral Oration," *Florilegium* 2 (1980):1–27; George Thomson, "From Religion to Philosophy," *Journal of Hellenic Studies* 73 (1953):77–83; Takis Poulakos, "Historiographies of the Tradition of Rhetoric: A Brief History of Classical Funeral Orations," *Western Journal of Speech Communication* 54 (Spring, 1990):172–88; ———, "The Historical Intervention of Gorgias' *Epitaphios*: The Genre of Funeral Oration and the Athenian Institution of Public Burials," *Pretext* 1–2 (1989):90–99; John E. Ziolkowski, *Thucydides and the Tradition of Funeral Speeches at Athens* (Salem, NH: The Ayer Company, 1981); and Theodore C. Burgess, *Epideictic Literature* (Chicago: University of Chicago Press, 1902). More recently Michael F. Carter, "The Ritual Functions of Epideictic Rhetoric: The Case of Socrates' Funeral Oration," *Rhetorica* 3 (1991) advances the claim that: "epideictic may be understood as ritual, indeed that epideictic is successful insofar as it achieves the qualities of ritual" (211). Although I believe Carter's conception of epideictic is insufficiently narrowed and his view of ritual unfortunately based on contemporary religious theorists, his discussion of the speech is valuable.

13. Aristotle, *Rhetoric*, 1.9; and, *Rhetoric to Alexander*, 3.

14. Loraux, *Invention*, 1.

15. Pericles delivered an oration at the end of the Samian War in 440 B.C. Only references to this speech remain in *Plutarch's Lives: The Translation Called Dryden's*, rev. A. H. Clough (Boston: Little

Brown and Co., 1881), 1.329, and in Aristotle, *Rhetoric*, 1.7.34. In the *Menexenus* (234B–236A) Plato refers to orations by Archinus and Dion. Menander mentions orations by Aristides in *Rhetores Graeci*, ed. L. Spengel (Leipzig: B. G. Teubner, 1899), 3.418–22. The texts of the speeches I have used in this study are: *Thucydides*, trans. Charles Foster Smith (London: William Heinemann, 1956); *Demosthenes*, trans. N. W. and N. J. Dewitt (London: William Heinemann, 1948), 3; "Gorgias," trans. George Kennedy in Sprague, *The Older Sophists*, 48–49; "Hyperides," in *Minor Attic Orators*, trans. J. O. Burtt, 2 (London: William Heinemann, 1954); *Lysias*, trans. W. R. M. Lamb (London: William Heinemann, 1960); and *Plato*, trans. R. G. Bury (London: William Heinemann, 1961), 7.

16. Poulakos, "Historiographies," 173.
17. George Thomson, "From Religion to Philosophy," *Journal of Hellenic Studies* 73 (1953):81. To maintain consistency of key terms and my announced intention of avoiding the use of unnecessary Greek terms I have omitted Thomson's inclusion of Greek equivalents and substituted "lament" for his word, "dirge."
18. Ziolkowski, *Thucydides*, 51ff.
19. Cf. Aristotle, *Rhetoric*, 1.5. Also Burgess, *Epideictic*, 120.
20. Poulakos, "Historiographies," 177.
21. Walters, "Rhetoric," 2.
22. Walters, "Rhetoric," 2.
23. Pseudo-Dionysius, *Ars Rhetorica I: Part VI, Methodos epitaphion*, in *Dionysii Halicarnasei Opuscula*, eds. H. Vrener and L. Radermacher, 6:277–83 (Leipzig: B. G. Teubner, 1904–1929). And Menander, *Rhetores*, 3:418–22. See for example James A. Mackin, Jr., "Schismogenesis and Community: Pericles' Funeral Oration," *The Quarterly Journal of Speech* 77 (August, 1991):251–62. Mackin argues the claim that "the epideictic rhetoric of Athens, as typified by the genre of funeral orations, built the community of Athens at the expense of the larger community of city-states. After the collapse of relations between the city-states, Athens ended up alone and defeated" (258).
24. Ziolkowski, *Thucydides*, 40 and Burgess, *Epideictic*, 148.
25. Ziolkowski, *Thucydides*, 40.
26. In addition to the speeches themselves I am indebted to the analyses provided by Ziolkowski, *Thucydides*, 58–72 and Burgess, *Epideictic*, 116ff.
27. Extensive lists of these commonplaces (e.g., "their death is noble and courageous, they endured dnagers, their fame is immortal," etc.) are readily accessible in Ziolkowski, *Thucydides*, 134–35 and Burgess, *Epideictic*, 156ff.

28. Burgess, *Epideictic*, 157.
29. *Webster's Third New International Dictionary*, 1323.
30. Theodore W. Jennings, Jr., "Liturgy," in *The Encyclopedia of Religion*, ed. Mircea Eliade, vol. 8, 580 (New York: Macmillan Publishing Co., 1987).
31. Jennings, "Liturgy," 580–83.
32. Jennings, "Liturgy," 582.
33. Jennings, "Liturgy," 582.
34. Aristotle, *Rhetoric*, 2.15.
35. Aristotle, *Rhetoric*, 2.15.

Chapter Five

Roman Funerals

Cultural Differences Between Greece and Rome

Many factors impinge upon and influence the specific ways in which funeral rituals are structured. Among these multiple factors one must address the beliefs in an afterlife held by pre-existing and coexisting cultures; the relationship of an individual to the collective at large; socio-political structures; and the taken-for-granted, unarguable social values from which every culture derives its fundamental defining characteristics. To understand, let alone appreciate, the several types of Roman funeral ceremonies, each with its attendant symbolic behaviors, some discussion of Roman cultural beliefs and practices is needed.

An interested reader can profit from any number of excellent histories of Rome.[1] However, given the purpose of this study, a retelling of the story of Rome, while valuable in its own right, would be an unnecessary digression. Only those factors that play a significant role in the funeral rituals need be entered into the argument. Indeed, many of the symbolic behaviors and their juxtaposition into oppositional elements bear a striking similarity to those already analyzed in the chapters on the funeral ceremonies in Greece. These similarities will be noted but not redeveloped. Instead, the focus in the ensuing sections of this chapter will be to concentrate attention on the unusual, the different, and the dissimilar symbolic behaviors in the Roman funerals and to explain how these distinctive behaviors function rhetorically to induce consolation in those affected by an individual's death.

More so than any other factor influencing the Roman funeral ceremony were the cultural beliefs and practices of the Etruscans, the "first urban and highly civilized people of Italy."[2] Long established on the Iberian peninsula before the origins of a Roman civilization, the Etruscans had burial customs for which "Rome was deeply and permanently indebted."[3] Basing his claim on archaeological evidence, J. M. C. Toynbee reaches this conclusion about the Etruscans.

> No other people has displayed a greater preoccupation—not to say—obsession—with man's fate at and after death. None has been more lavish in providing, in the terms of life, for the soul's life beyond the grave, whether that life was conceived of as lived in the tomb itself or in some invisible, probably subterranean, realm of the deceased. For, wherever the dead dwelt, their condition was clearly believed to resemble that of the living very closely and to require the surroundings and amenities (food, vessels for cooking, eating, and drinking, toilet articles, arms, armor, and the like, either real or counterfeited in art) that had been familiar to them in their mundane existence.[4]

Since the Etruscans held a fixed belief in an idyllic afterlife,[5] one can anticipate, with a degree of certainty, the use of more symbolic behaviors in the marginalization and aggregation phases of a funeral ritual than in the separation phase. Personal and collective loss would occur, to be sure, as does grief and social displacement but the symbolic work of an Etruscan collective would be directed toward keeping the dead person alive in his or her new state of existence. Consolation, for the collective, is achieved by an amplified emphasis on certain of the oppositional symbolic elements and a diminished inclusion of others. In other words, oppositional elements that rhetorically construct and privilege the future vis-à-vis the past or present will be featured.

Another cultural difference that both distinguishes Rome from Greece and reflects itself in the funeral ceremony is the relationship of an individual to the collective, the Roman citizen to Rome. Although the two cultures interacted and complimented each other in numerous ways,[6] the members of a Greek polis were essentially inhabitants of a city. The concept of a Roman citizen (*civis*) connotes "the idea of the family, an outsider admitted into the family, a guest or a friend."[7] A Roman, therefore, belonged to a "sacral and political community based on a community of rights (*jus civile*, citizen's rights) which, among other things, strictly regulated family ties."[8]

For most contemporary readers, no doubt, the term family denotes a relatively small social unit. A citizen of Rome, however, not only belonged to what we would recognize as a nuclear family, but also a clan (*gens*), a large social group interrelated by blood and marriage relationships and headed by a single, legally powerful leader, the father of the family (*pater familias*). Rome, itself, was considered the father, the parent (*patria*). Like a parent, Rome protected its citizens, its family, with its laws and military. Like a responsible family member, a citizen strengthened the State via loyalty, various forms of tribute, and military service.

In Rome, then, with citizenship inextricably connected to familiar relationships, a death would have—or could have—far-reaching consequences. Consolation for the collective would need to take precedence over consolation for the immediate, and most closely related survivors. The fears and uncertainties of social displacement, disjuncture, and disorganization brought about by the death of a family member would create a rhetorical situation, the resolution of which must both reassure and reinforce. The symbolic and suasive behaviors in a funeral ritual would need to restore confidence in the social order and persuade those affected by the death to trust in the continuation of the social life of the civic institutions. Death's fracturing challenge need be countered with persuasive languages of enduring strength and unity.

A Roman, by virtue of birth or law, was not only a citizen but, by virtue of wealth, also a member of a social class: the least wealthy and most numerous, the plebians; those with wealth but not born into a noble family, the knights; and, those with wealth and noble lineage, the most powerful and least numerous, the patricians.[9] In short, Rome was a timocracy. Consequently, an individual's funeral ceremony would depend, in a large part, on the financial resources available to the survivors. Not only observable differences in the comparative scale of the ceremonies but the audiences for the funeral rituals would differ. A wealthy aristocrat's funeral, for example, conceivably would have multiple publics and, quite probably, functions other than consolation as well. Wealthy citizens of Rome historically accepted greater financial responsibilities in the State than the poorer citizens and the fact that their funerals would be more grand and more spectacular ought to come as no surprise.

Intertwined with Rome's citizenship and timocratic structures were the unquestioned cultural values which, in turn, help explain some of the symbolic behaviors used in the funeral ceremonies. Derived from the traditional moral code on which Roman law was based, the notion of virtue (*virtus*) was clearly fundamental, central, and pervasive. Vastly different from any contemporary understanding of the term, virtue, for a Roman, was a way of life. "[*Virtus*] included everything which made up the true man and a useful member of society. It is virtue, says the poet Lucilius (ca. 180–103 B.C.), for a man to know what is good, what evil, what useless, shameful, and dishonorable; to be an enemy of bad men and customs, to be a friend and protector of those that are good; to place first one's country's good, next that of one's parents, and last that of one's self."[10] The hierarchy of values and responsibilities as well as the injunctions about the very nature of good and evil is encompassed in Roman *virtus*. Insofar as some Roman funerals employed eulogies, the bases on which the deceased might be praised can be located in the ways one lived in accord with *virtus*.

Four other cultural values play varying degrees of importance on the conduct of a Roman funeral ceremony: piety, trustworthiness, gravity, and constancy. Piety "implied devotion and loyalty to the family group and a willing acceptance of parental authority, which gave unity and strength to the family. It further meant reverence and devotion to the gods as members of the family *as shown in action* by the exact performance of all required religious rites and ceremonies."[11] With a cultural value such as piety operating as a directional guide, one would anticipate, at moments when the Roman family is most seriously challenged—the death of one of its members—that action languages would be employed. Deeds, not words, display piety.

The degree to which a deceased Roman had lived in accord with the remaining three values—trustworthiness, gravity, and constancy—become the substantive matter for eulogy. To praise a deceased Roman before an audience of Romans, all of whom possessed an incontestable belief in these values, offered a funeral orator a relatively easy task: recite and recount instances wherein the deceased performed his obligations (trustworthiness), displayed self-control (gravity), and persevered in the face of trying circumstances (constancy). For an audience, then, the voicing of a dead person's record of actions would link, enthymematically, to their preexisting value system and any conclusion, if it need even be stated explicitly, would be a variant of "this person lived as a Roman and deserves our regard, respect, care, and esteem." In a later section of this chapter, the placement and substance of the Roman funeral speech of praise (*laudatio funebris*) will be discussed in more detail.

One final cultural difference between Greece and Rome, a difference that accounts for a significant change in Rome's funeral practice, is the change in political institutions that the country underwent. Initially Rome was a Monarchy (700 B.C.– 500 B.C.), then a Republic (500 B.C.–27 B.C.), and then an Empire (27 B.C.–476 B.C.). As each of these political changes took place, developed, flourished, and declined, funeral rituals predictably changed. Death, however, whether of an ordinary and poor Roman citizen, a wealthy aristocrat, or later an emperor, continued to be a grief-provoking event. To console a surviving family, clan, or an empire required the use of cultural rituals, rituals containing symbols whose rhetorical function was to persuade those affected that the deceased lives and that the living collectivity will continue. Accordingly, an analysis of persuasion in the funeral ritual of an ordinary citizen is in order.

The Citizen's Funeral

Archaeological and literary evidence for the conduct of an ordinary person's funeral ritual is less abundant than those of aristocrats and emperors. This observation is not surprising since writers are more apt to record the extraordinary and the wealthy families could afford expensive materials and sculptors for their tombs and mausoleums. Nonetheless, the traditional funeral (*funus translaticum*) contained features quite similar to those of the Archaic Greeks as well as several unusual and distinctively Roman ones.[12] To avoid needless repetition the ritual will be described in full, but only the distinctive features need be analyzed.

When a Roman was about to die his or her relatives and friends gathered privately to comfort, grieve, and fulfill their duty of piety owed to the dead. The closest relative gave the dying person a final kiss and closed the dead person's eyes. Those assembled shouted the dead person's name and began their lament. The body was then washed, annointed, and dressed. A coin was placed "in the mouth to pay the deceased's fare in Charon's barque,"[13] and the body was then displayed on a funeral bed in the home. After several days, the mourners, dressed in black and led by torch bearers, moved in procession to the site of burial or cremation outside the city. Grave goods of various kinds were placed with the remains and a procession back to the home followed. "On returning from the funeral the relatives had to undergo the *suffitio*, a rite of purification by fire and water. On the same day there began a period cleansing ceremonies (*feriae denicales*) held at the deceased's house; and again on the same day a funerary feast, the *silicornium*, was later at the grave in honor of the dead. There was also the *cena novendialis* eaten at the grave on the ninth day after the funeral, at the end of the period of full mourning."[14] Thus, the traditional funeral for a Roman concluded.

From this admittedly brief sketch one can easily recognize the many symbolic behaviors quite similar to those used in the Archaic Greek funeral and discussed in chapter 3. The dissimilar action and object languages invite attention, namely, the final kiss, the closing of the deceased's eyes, the shout, the placing of a coin, and the use of torch bearers in the funeral march. All, except the latter, occur in the separation phase of the funeral rite from which one can conclude that death, for the Roman family, required a greater effort at consoling the survivors than in the marginalization or aggregation phases. With the Roman's belief in an afterlife such an observation ought not be surprising. Distancing the dead person from the living is the rhetorical function of symbolic behaviors of separation. The living, with the kiss, the shout, the closing of the eyes, and placement of the coin, symbolically divorce themselves from the deceased. The kiss, an act of human affection, is given, but not returned. The shout, a verbal act inviting a reciprocating verbal answer, is met with silence. Living individuals see, apprehend, and recognize; the dead no longer share the most valued human sense of sight. The living can view the body; the deceased, with closed eyes, cannot. The living carry their money in purses or in their hands; the dead, devoid of movement, carry it in their immobile mouth. The dichotomy and disjuncture between the living and the dead is rhetorically reinforced by these oppositions. Insofar as accepting the death of a loved one is the beginning of the grief process, the symbolic behaviors of separation, for the Romans, function suasively to console. By employing action and object languages rhetorically designed to detach the dead from the living the Roman family would be well prepared for the remaining phases of the funeral ritual.

One might easily discount the use of torches in the Roman funeral procession and explain the fact as a necessary element for night burials. For a time funeral processions and burials were done at night and, obviously, light would be needed. Yet, when the processions and burials became traditionally conducted during the day, torch bearers continued in use. How might this be explained?

The phenomenon of fire, for the Romans, was a reality inspiring worship.[15] Vulcan was the Italian god of fire and of the art of forging and smelting. Shrines were erected in his honor, festivals held, and temples built. Fire, as a fact of nature, was both friend and foe, boon and bane. When controlled, fire warmed, lighted, and aided; uncontrolled, fire devastated and destroyed. As a symbol, fire could be both light and life as well as destruction and death. Few symbols have the richness of ambiguity that fire has. When used as a significant feature in the Roman funeral procession the lighted torches, therefore, are equally rich in rhetorical impact. The living control the torches; the deceased, like the flame, is controlled. Flames move; the deceased is moved. Torches dispel darkness; the deceased is carried into darkness. The mourners, as a collective, share the beneficial effects of the flames; the deceased is ushered toward his or her new state of existence with a visual symbol denoting both life and death. Rhetorically, the torch lighted procession along with the other symbolic behaviors of marginalization, work to take the living to the edge of life and the dead to the threshold of their new state of existence. Boundaries are symbolically and actually established.

The Aristocrat's Funeral

When one contrasts the simplicity and private character of the traditional Roman's funeral to the lavish complexity and public format of the ritual used for the Roman aristocracy, a contemporary reader might well experience revulsion. Comparing the wealthy Roman's funeral to the Athenian State ceremony, Loraux expresses no little disgust. "Such funerals," she says, "were the preserve of an elite and were not so much public as a form of publicity: an exhibition of the omnipotence of the *gentes*, not a civic celebration."[16] The interpretation of the aristocratic funeral ritual in this section will differ from Loraux's primarily because she analyzes funeral rites from a political, not a consolation-producing, set of criteria. Claude Nicolet, in his book *The World of the Citizen in Republican Rome*, also differs from Loraux's assessment. He sees the aristocratic funeral as "a pledge of a certain social order and also an opportunity for the public, represented by throngs of clients mustered for the occasion, to associate itself with the ostentatious rivalries of great families. For a long time exhibitions of this kind actually meant . . . an exaltation of the nation's unity in the persons of its great men."[17] As a civilization Rome was based on display and spectacle both of which are at direct odds with the usual moral tenets of contemporary readers enculturated with Judeo-Christian values. Nonetheless, individual and collective grief, loss, uncertainty, disruption, fear, etc. — all the human reactions and emotions experienced at the death of a loved one — would affect the members of a wealthy Roman family and the interrelated clan, arguably, even more so than plebian families of more modest means.

What, then, happened at an aristocrat's funeral and how was consolation rhetorically constructed? In the absence of direct evidence to the contrary one can safely assume that the activities immediately following the death of an aristocrat were the same, or essentially the same, as those in an ordinary ritual. The ceremony takes on markedly different features from the time of displaying the body to its final disposal.

The body was displayed on an elaborately decorated and elevated couch atop of which were two mattresses.[18] Flaming torches were placed around the bier adorned with fruit, flowers, and incense. Hired mourners, musicians, and relatives dressed in black surrounded the display, a display that could last for seven days. Near the end of the laying out phase heralds were sent out to announce the death and summon the citizens to the funeral. The historian, Polybius (204 B.C.–122 B.C.) describes the next phase of the ritual.

> Whenever any illustrious man dies, he is carried at his funeral into the forum to the so-called rostra, sometimes conspicuous in an upright posture and more rarely reclined. Here with all the people standing round, a grown-up son, if he has left one who happens to be present, or if not some other relative mounts the rostra and discourses on the virtues and successful achievements of the dead. As a consequence the multitude and not only those who had a part in these achievements, but those also who had none, when the facts are recalled to their minds and brought before their eyes, are moved to such sympathy that the loss seems to be not confined to the mourners, but a public one affecting the whole people. Next after the interment and the performance of the usual ceremonies, they place the image of the departed in the most conspicuous position in the house, enclosed in a wooden shrine. This image is a mask reproducing with remarkable fidelity both the features and complexion of the deceased. On the occasion of public sacrifices they display these images, and decorate them with much care, and when any distinguished member of the family dies they take them to the funeral, putting them on men who seem to them to bear the closest resemblance to the original in stature and carriage. These representatives wear togas, with a purple border if the deceased was a consul or praetor, whole purple if he was a censor, and embroidered with gold if he had celebrated a triumph or achieved anything similar. They all ride in chariots preceded by the fasces, axes, and other insignia by which the different magistrates were wont to be accompanied according to the respective dignity of the offices of state held by each during his life; and when they arrive at the rostra they all seat themselves in a row on ivory chairs. There could not easily be a more ennobling spectacle for a young man who aspires to fame and virtue. For who would not be inspired by the sight of the images of men renowned for their excellence, all together as if alive and breathing? What spectacle could be

more glorious than this? Besides, he who makes the oration over the man about to be buried, when he has finished speaking of him recounts the successes and exploits of the rest whose images are present, beginning from the most ancient. By this means, by this constant renewal of the good report of brave men, the celebrity of those who performed noble deeds is rendered immortal, while at the same time the fame of those who did good service to their country becomes known to the people and a heritage for future generations. But the most important result is that young men are thus inspired to endure every suffering for the public welfare in the hope of winning the glory that attends on brave men.[19]

From the Forum the funeral procession moved to the site of inhumation or cremation. Aristocrats were either buried in ornately carved sarcophagi or cremated. If the latter option was used, "the eyes of the deceased were opened when it was placed on the pyre along with various gifts and some of the deceased's personal possessions."[20] Those in attendance again shouted the person's name, the pyre was ignited, and later, the remains placed in a suitably rich container and buried. Thereafter the usual purifications, banquets, and anniversary commemorations ensued.

Without doubt the embellished and ornamented display of an aristocrat's funeral served functions other than consolation: reinforcing cultural values necessary for the continued existence of the State, visually fortifying the political position and power of the clan, and competing in an arena of ostentation with other clans. Nevertheless, those affected, directly or indirectly, by the death (recall that for the Romans with their patron-client arrangements and interlocked, extended family systems the numbers could be quite significant) would experience grief. The death of a patrician, a wealthy public officer who controlled the affairs of many individuals, would arouse anxieties, concerns, and worries which, if left unaddressed could weaken or destroy the social and political relationships needed for the continued functioning of the group and, by extension, the group as a part of Rome. Here, consolation need be targeted as much or more at comforting and consoling the collective as relieving grief from a personal loss. The scale alone of an aristocrat's funeral flies in the face of the cultural values of gravity and constancy. The death of a patrician appears to be the cause for a public celebration and the apparent contradiction is best resolved by viewing the ceremony from a rhetorical perspective.

The symbolic elements, juxtaposed in opposition, array themselves on polar loci of *public* over against private, *past* over against present, *power* over against impotence, and the *living collective* over against the deceased individual. In each instance the first term is affirmed, featured, and asserted; the second term, minimized.

In an aristocrat's funeral the impact of death is rapidly removed from the private sphere of the immediate nuclear family and made public through the action and object languages of the crier; the week-long viewing; and the processional detour to the Forum, the public space used for political meetings, judicial proceedings, and commercial traffic. The verbal invitation to the citizenry to join the funeral ceremony functions to enlarge the audience and, thereby, broadens the group actually or potentially affected with grief. The psychological consequences of death are shared by a public collectivity. Displaying the body for seven days permits, if not actually encourages, more people to participate in the separation phase. The sheer size of the attending public is a suasive message of consolation to the private, immediate family members. Halting the procession at the Forum reinforces the public, not private character of the patrician's funeral. The deceased belongs, not to the small grieving immediate family, but to the public, to the State, and to Rome. By diffusing and diluting individual grief, the rhetorical symbols of publicness are set in opposition to the singleness of the deceased. Within the separation phase of the ritual, then, the deceased becomes, rhetorically, not a visual reminder causing sorrow and pain but an object causing a large, living collective to gather, participate, and share in the work of the cultural ritual.

An individual afflicted with grief, as discussed in chapter 2, tends to be overcome with past memories and fears of the future. The funeral ritual for a Roman aristocrat rhetorically reconstructs the deceased's past in a celebratory drama that glorifies the past to dismiss the future. Before the assembled public, typically the deceased's son—a living reminder of the dead person's past—delivers the funeral speech (*laudatio funebris*). The very structure of the address revisions the past: meritorious deeds and achievements of the deceased are chronicled and then the illustrious deeds and achievements of the ancestors of the deceased are recited. Masks, replicas of celebrated personages from the deceased's past, joined with the visual symbols of political ranks and offices held by the deceased's ancestors all send a clear message that the past prevails. Acts of *virtus*, morally good deeds and services done in the past and done for Rome, deserve display, recognition, acclaim, and celebration by Rome. No laments and no expressions of sorrow appear. No concern for the future is expressed in the rubric within The Forum.

Significant also is the comparatively quick movement to aggregation in the aristocratic ritual. By juxtaposing the deceased vis-à-vis his ancestors in the funeral speech and the deceased's visage over against the parade of ancestral masks a rhetorical conclusion is asserted: the deceased has now joined company with his collectivity of honored and honorable ancestors and his praiseworthy accomplishments will remain alive, present, and extant so long as the clan and Rome survive.

Were all this insufficient, the power of the living collectivity would be repeatedly and symbolically juxtaposed with the impotence of the deceased to replace, rhetorically, anguish with awe, helplessness with strength, and the dread of mortality with a guarantee of immortality. Surrounding the lifeless and immobile corpse, the aristocratic ritual places numerous symbols of power and superiority. Large numbers of attendants visit the expensively decorated bier; dignitaries ride in chariots; public officials are seated on ivory chairs in the forum; and the remains are housed in costly and near permanent tombs. A person's death, if the person were a Roman aristocrat, was a phenomena calling forth a symbol system of redefinition, celebration, and control.

The Emperor's Funeral

Few contemporary analogies exist by which to comprehend or begin to appreciate the funeral ceremony of a Roman Emperor.[21] The illustration of the national rites accorded John F. Kennedy and Martin Luther King in chapter 2 do not begin to compare with the size, complexity, and impact of the Roman ritual. Attending our modern Olympic Games and observing the ceremonies as a spectator might well be the closest approximation—albeit of an entirely different order—to witnessing an emperor's funeral. Best described as a ritual nested within a spectacle, the Imperial ceremony adds a significant dimension to those already discussed in this book, the concept of spectacle itself.

"Of all the genres of cultural performance," notes anthropologist John MacAloon, "the spectacle is the least well known."[22] Nonetheless, certain defining traits can be identified. In a spectacle, symbolic codes and the sense of sight are predominant. That which is viewed must be impressive in size and grandeur and the roles of actor and audience are required for the cultural performance. "Spectacle is a dynamic form, demanding movement, action, change, and exchange on the part of human actors who are center stage, and the spectators must be excited in turn."[23] Frank Manning, who essentially agrees with MacAloon's definition, adds a useful distinction: "Whereas traditional ritual temporarily suspends but ultimately validates the principles of social structure, modern performance genres have the capacity to subvert the system and formulate alternatives. Such phenomena as spectacles impose their symbolism on social processes and often exert a major influence on the direction of those processes. Life follows performance."[24] The Roman Imperial funeral clearly fulfills each of these necessary and sufficient conditions for spectacle.

Combining a consolatory ritual with a spectacle results in a cultural performance with an unmistakable rhetorical message of unsurpassable power, mastery, and control. While an aristocrat's funeral featured symbols reifying the past vis-à-vis the present, Imperial funerals used symbols to resignify the present over against the future. By incorporating some features of the aristocrat's funeral—masks and an oration—an emperor's ritual could be viewed as a recognizable cultural ritual. The ceremony, as we shall see, accomplishes consolation with a host of new symbols designed to address the exigence of an emperor's death.

From Augustus, the first Roman Emperor in A.D. 14 to Con-
stantine in A.D. 337, Rome was ruled by sixty emperors, auto-
cratic sovereigns with total control over millions of people and
dozens of countries. Whether benevolent or savage, competent
or ludicrous during their reign, emperors, at death, occasioned
a time of grief and major social disruption. The emotional experience of loss at the death of an aristocrat may well have been
widespread and public, but "grief at an imperial death was even
more strongly displayed. At the death in AD 19 of Germanicus,
Tiberius's heir, 'the populace stoned temples and upset altars
of the gods; people threw their household deities into the
streets and exposed their new-born children,' while at the
death of the emperor Otho (AD 69) some of his soldiers commit-
ted suicide at the pyre. Life was hardly worth living any-
more."[25] An emperor's death was of such magnitude that
officials dressed in the apparel of those lower in social rank, all
civic business halted, temples closed, and, in some cases, a year
long period of mourning was decreed. An emperor's death was
the death of a father, not the father of a clan, but of the entire
country.

Imperial funerals were staged in the Forum and moved, in
procession, a mile away to the Campus Martius, a site on which
political meetings, military exercises, and public entertain-
ments were held. Cassius Dio (A.D. 155–A.D. 230) a Greek historian and a member of the Roman Senate, was a participant
and spectator at the funeral of Pertinax (A.D. 193). He records
the sequence of events in this way:

> His funeral, in spite of the time that had elapsed since his
> death, was carried out as follows. In the Roman Forum a
> wooden platform was constructed hard by the marble ros-
> tra, upon which was set a shrine, without walls, but sur-
> rounded by columns, cunningly wrought of both ivory and
> gold. In it there was placed a bier of the same materials,
> surrounded by heads of both land and sea animals and
> adorned with coverlets of purple and gold. Upon this
> rested an effigy of Pertinax in wax, laid out in triumphal
> garb; and a comely youth was keeping the flies away from
> it with peacock feathers, as though it were really a person
> sleeping. While the body lay there in state, Severus as well

as we senators and our wives approached, wearing
mourning; the women sat in the porticos, and we men under the open sky. After this there moved past, first, images of all the famous Romans of old, then choruses of
boys and men, singing a dirge-like hymn to Pertinax;
there followed all the subject nations, represented by
bronze figures attired in native dress, and the guilds of
the City itself—those of the lictors, the scribes, the heralds, and all the rest. Then came images of other men who
had been distinguished for some exploit or invention or
manner of life. Behind these were the cavalry and infantry in armour, the race-horses, and all the funeral offerings that the emperor and we (senators) and our wives,
the more distinguished knights, and communities, and
the corporations of the City, had sent. Following them
came an altar gilded all over and adorned with ivory and
gems of India. When these had passed by, Severus
mounted the rostra and read a eulogy of Pertinax. We
shouted our approval many times in the course of his address, now praising and now lamenting Pertinax, but our
shouts were loudest when he concluded. Finally, when the
bier was about to be moved, we all lamented and wept
together. It was brought down from the platform by the
high priests and the magistrates, not only those who were
actually in office at the time but also those who had been
elected for the ensuing year; and they gave it to certain
knights to carry. All the rest of us, now, marched ahead of
the bier, some beating our breasts and others playing a
dirge on the flute, but the emperor followed behind all the
rest; and in this order we arrived at the Campus Martius.
There a pyre had been built in the form of a tower having
three stories and adorned with ivory and gold as well as a
number of statues, while on its very summit was placed a
gilded chariot that Pertinax had been wont to drive. Inside
this pyre the funeral offerings were cast and the bier was
placed in it, and then Severus and the relatives of Pertinax kissed the effigy. The emperor then ascended a tri-
bunal, while we, the senate, except the magistrates, took
our places on wooden stands in order to view the ceremonies both safely and conveniently. The magistrates and

the equestrian order, arrayed in a manner befitting their station, and likewise the cavalry and the infantry, passed in and out around the pyre performing intricate evolutions, both those of peace and those of war. Then at last the consuls applied fire to the structure, and when this had been done, an eagle flew aloft from it. Thus was Pertinax made immortal.[26]

From this rich description one can easily see the use of symbols placed in opposition to persuade a collectivity, in this case an empire, to accept death, and to be comforted with a reassurance of future life—their own, the empire, and the emperor.

Most obvious, perhaps, in the separation phase are the symbols arrayed over against the deceased's body which is silent, immobile, small, sightless, and singular. The silent corpse (more about the effigy later) is juxtaposed with the sounds of laments, the sounds of thousands parading to the bier, the speech, the shouts, and the massed weeping. An immobile corpse is juxtaposed with a moving parade of dignitaries and groups each of which can be read as representing the many economic, political, and social dimensions of Rome. Against the smallness and singularity of the corpse is juxtaposed a huge cast of participants all together proclaiming, symbolically, that death is not as great as the collective.

In the visual arena, the territory of spectacle itself, the sightlessness of the corpse is minimalized, if not actually dismissed, by sights of grandeur and magnificence. A columnar shrine, royal trappings of precious metals and colors, displays of taxidermy denoting total mastery over the animal kingdom, mourners in special dress, ancestral statues, bronze figures, the display of an armed military—all this acts to separate, through rhetorically placed visual symbols, the deceased from the living.

In the marginalization phase of the rite, a phase that must have taken considerable time to traverse the distance, a significant reversal occurs. In all the other funeral ceremonies thus far considered in this book, the bier leads the collective dance. Here, the deceased is placed at the rear of the procession. The ambiguity of symbols, action, and object languages can be observed here. When successful Roman generals were granted a triumph, a formalized victory celebration and parade ensued in which the general came last in order of march. Within the funeral ceremony the deceased emperor's placement in the procession, symbolically, can rhetorically unite the dead ruler to a living conqueror, one defeated by death to one victorious in life. By locating the bier behind the cortege one can also interpret the symbolic act as denoting a position of power—the deceased as directing even in death those yet alive. High ranking religious and political officials carried (were placed under) the bier, a symbolic act denoting the same power relationship that obtained during the life of the emperor. Within the marginalization phase, therefore, the deceased both begins the shift to a new state of spiritual existence, to be sure, but also retains, through a rhetoric of symbols, certain attributes—power, command, and domination—held in the previous living state.

From the spectators' viewpoint the Imperial funeral in all its splendid majesty had to be perceived as a fiction-treated-as-fact counterposed to fact. That is, the abundant representations or symbolic features of the effigy and the ancestral masks, the bronze figures of all subject nations, offered more than visual reminders and associative connections. During the spectacle in the Forum the effigy, a regally garbed and iconic representation of the deceased, was treated as factual, sleeping, and as one alive and requiring a personal attendant. The metallic representations of foreign nations, too, were treated as fact, as requiring appropriate and identifiable clothing. All of the fictional aspects, however, are associated with death and absence. The emperor and his ancestors are gone and, in the spectacle, fictionalized. The representatives of foreign, conquered nations are physically absent and also fictionalized via identifiable costume. These fictions-treated-as-facts—when placed within the action, movement, and exchange of the living and present "factual" components of the spectacle—could only add to the tremendous excitement of the ceremony turned celebration. The presence, placement, and actions of the dignitaries, for the spectators, are real and also symbols of Rome's political power. The cavalry and infantry, marching and maneuvering, in full battle dress are not only living and present, but, in the aggregate, an imposing symbol of Rome's strength, the spectator's real protectors. An eagle flying from atop the

pyre is both real and a visual symbol of the emperor's soul en-
route to a new and eternal life.[27]

For the Romans an Imperial funeral was a ritual wrapped
in a spectacle. Ritual demands those partaking to act and attend to the ceremony for its efficacy. "Ritual is a duty, spectacle
is a choice."[28] Rhetoric, of course, works best when optionality
and choice are present, consequently, consoling the collective
survivors of an imperial death is accomplished in two ways: as
traditional participants in a funeral ritual and as audience
members at a staged, lavish spectacle. Whether participant or
audience the rhetorical message is the same: the deceased lives
and the living are reassured and reunited.

NOTES

1. A small selection of books relevant to this chapter would include:
   E. Guhl and W. Koner, *Everyday Life of the Greeks and Romans*
   (New York: Crescent Books, 1989), 591–96; Thomas Wiedemann,
   Adults and Children in the Roman Empire (London: Routledge,
   1989); *Roman Civilization*, eds. Naphtali Lewis and Meyer Rein-
   hold (New York: Harper and Row Publishing Co., 1966); *Sources
   for Ancient History*, ed. Michael Crawford (New York: Cambridge
   University Press, 1983); Charles W. Fornara, *The Nature of History in Ancient Greece and Rome* (Berkeley: University of California Press, 1983); Alan Wardman, *Rome's Debt to Greece* (New York:
   St. Martin's Press, 1976); Sue Blundell, *The Origins of Civilization in Greek and Roman Thought* (London: Croom Helm, 1986);
   and Barry Baldwin, *Studies on Late Roman and Byzantine History, Literature, and Language* (Amsterdam: J. C. Gieben Pub.,
   1984).
2. Fritz M. Heichelheim and Cedric A. Yeo, *A History of the Roman
   People* (Engelwood Cliffs, NJ: Prentice-Hall, Inc., 1962), 26.
3. J. M. C. Toynbee, *Death and Burial in the Roman World* (Ithaca,
   NY: Cornell University Press, 1971), 11.
4. Toynbee, *Death*, 11.
5. Tomb paintings of the afterlife from the fifth and sixth centuries
   contain themes of "feasting, fishing and fowling, athletic games,
   horsemanship, dancing, and music." Toynbee, *Death*, 12.
6. M. J. Cary and T. J. Haarhoff, *Life and Thought in the Greek and
   Roman World* (London: Methuen and Co., Ltd., rep. 1968), v–vi.
7. Claude Nicolet, *The World of the Citizen in Republican Rome*,

trans. P. S. Falla (Berkeley: University of California Press, 1988), 22.

8. Nicolet, *World*, 23.

9. Nicolet describes the latter two social classes in this way:

> This was the sphere of the 'political class,' consisting essentially of the magistrates and promagistrates (about 50 persons at most in any given year), the Senate (300 members, afterwards 500 or 600, mostly ex-magistrates who expected to hold high office again), and, from 123 BC, a few hundred equites who were on the panel of jurymen. This very small collection of people—an oligarchy in the strict etymological sense—constituted the Roman political class in combination with what may be called their entourage: friends or relatives from the senatorial or equestrian class who had chosen to stay out of the limelight and not go into politics on their own account—Atticus is a typical example—or else members of the dependent classes: clients, freedmen and even slaves. These associates might actually be the moving force behind a given policy, either as the drafters of texts or as managers of the financial interests of their friends and patrons (e.g. the celebrated Philotimus). (383)

10. Heichelheim and Yeo, *History*, 74.

11. Heichelheim and Yeo, *History*, 74, emphasis mine.

12. Cf. Toynbee, *Death*, ch. 3.

13. Toynbee, *Death*, 44. Also, Juvenal, *Satires*, 3.267.

14. Toynbee, *Death*, 50.

15. Cf. the Prometheus legend in Hesiod's *Theogony*.

16. Loraux, 43.

17. Nicolet, *World*, 347.

18. A more detailed reconstruction of the *funus publicum* along with supportive citations from literary sources can be read in Toynbee, *Death*, 44–45.

19. *Polybius: The Histories*, trans. W. R. Patton (New York: G. P. Putnam's Sons, 1927), 6.53–54. Cf. Cicero, *Pro Milone*, 13.33, and *de Oratore*, 2.84.

20. Toynbee, *Death*, 50ff.

21. Cf. S. R. F. Price, *Rituals and Power: The Roman Imperial Cult in Asia Minor* (New York: Cambridge University Press, 1984).

22. John J. MacAloon, "Olympic Games and the Theory of Spectacle in Modern Societies," in *Rite, Drama, Festival, Spectacle: Rehearsals Toward a Theory of Cultural Performance*, ed. John J. MacAloon, 243 (Philadelphia: The Institute for the Study of Human Issues, 1984).

23. MacAloon, "Olympic," 244.

24. Frank E. Manning, "Spectacle," in *International Encyclopedia of Communications*, ed. Erik Barnouw, vol. 4, 139 (New York: Oxford University Press, 1989).

25. Simon Price, "From Noble Funerals to Divine Cult: The Consecration of Roman Emperors," in *Rituals of Royalty: Power and Ceremonial in Traditional Societies*, eds. David Cannadine and Simon Price, 62–63 (New York: Cambridge University Press, 1987). Cf. Dio, 54.28.5.

26. *Dio's Roman History*, trans. Earnest Cary (New York: G. P. Putnam's Sons, 1928), 75.4–5.

27. Cf. Price's extensive discussion of apotheosis in "From Noble," 71ff.

28. MacAloon, "Olympic," 243.

Chapter Six

Consolatory Discourse

Two verbal forms of consolation, the Roman funeral speech and consolatory literature, remain for analysis before concluding this study. The first type deserves attention because the speech formed an integral part of every funeral. The second type, literary forms of consolation, might be regarded as inappropriate and irrelevant to the premise and focus of this book. Nonetheless, a brief discussion of literary consolatory practices is defensible because here and only here does the primary tool of rhetoric—arguing from probability—reemerge. The methods of urging a course of action developed by the Sophists in fifth century Greece (see chapter 4) fit the rhetorical situations in which one attempted to argue, in a written composition, that a bereaved individual should replace grief with reasoning or other emotional states. Written consolations also provide an insight into what were probably the more personal types of consolation actually spoken between and among mourners. Consequently, both verbal forms of consolation will be addressed.

Funeral Speeches

Although much is known about the speeches of praise used in the Roman funeral ceremony, no text of an actual public speech is extant. An absence of this kind can be partially overcome, however, with the historian's accounts that survive, the discussions of the funeral speech found in rhetorical treatises, and evidence from various fragments and inscriptions.[1] First, to the historians.

Plutarch (A.D. 50–A.D. 120) claims that the custom originated when Valerius Publicola delivered a funeral speech for Brutus, his co-consul. "The people applauded likewise the honours he did to his colleague, in adding to his obsequies a funeral oration: which was so much liked by the Romans, and found so good a reception that it became customary for the best men to celebrate the funerals of great citizens with speeches in their commendation: and their antiquity in Rome is affirmed to be greater than in Greece, unless, with the orator Anaximenes, we make Solon the first author."[2] Dionysius of Halicarnassus (ca. 30 B.C.) notes that the funeral oration was a relatively late development for the Athenians. He observes that, "for the Greeks, orations were given primarily for the war dead (some might have little other merit than dying in battle). But, the Romans believed the honor should go to all for the virtues they displayed in their lives."[3]

That the funeral speech was an act of honor is clear. The speech has as its rhetorical objective the ennobling and glorifying of the deceased based on what the deceased had achieved or done. The speech itself, then, was a public reward, a recognition of a distinguished life addressed to the funeral audience. Not only male aristocrats and emperors were accorded the honor of a funeral speech; a considerable number of women also received the recognition.[4]

Custom required that the funeral speech be given by the deceased's son or a close relative;[5] Roman piety would explain the obligation. Youth and inexperience, no doubt, created a need to formalize the pattern of the speech to reduce the difficulty of such a presentation. In other instances the designated speaker might be another magistrate, a consul, or the succeeding emperor but, regardless of political rank, the pattern was set and scrupulously followed. For the nature of this pattern we turn to the rhetoricians.

Cicero (106 B.C.–43 B.C.) comes close to removing the funeral speech from the compass of rhetoric. His near dismissal is significant in that he recognizes the unique constraints praising the dead impose. Placed as an observation of Antonius in the *de Oratore*, Cicero states: "But to my mind not everything that we say need be reduced to theory and rule. For from those same sources, whence the rules of speaking are all derived, we shall also be able to set off a funeral oration without feeling the want of those scholastic rudiments, since, even though no one were to teach these, is there a man who would not know the good points of a human being?"[6] One need only remember that the Roman funeral speech formed a part of a much larger ritual, a ritual whose symbol system rhetorically celebrated the deceased, life, the afterlife, and the living community, to appreciate the coercive and obligatory demands placed on the speaker. The community expects, the culture demands, and the ritual forces a speaker to praise the deceased. One needs only a list of promptuaries, topical headings susceptible to dilation, exemplification, and amplification to satisfy the requirements. These, too, Cicero readily enumerates:

> He who proposes to be the panegyrist of anyone will understand that he has in the first placed to deal fully with the favours of fortune. These are the advantages of race, wealth, connexions, friendships, power, good health, beauty, vigour, talent, and the rest of the attributes that are either physical or externally imposed: it must be explained that the person commended made a right use of these benefits if he possessed them, managed sensibly without them, if they were denied to him, and bore the loss with resignation, if they were taken away from him; and after that the speaker will marshal instances of conduct, either active or passive, on the part of the subject of his praises; whereby he manifested wisdom, generosity, valour, righteousness, greatness of soul, sense of duty, gratitude, kindliness or, in short, any moral excellence you please. These and similar indications of character the would-be panegyrist will readily discern.[7]

Equipped with this checklist a speaker could navigate, with some confidence, the situational barriers. Additional help was offered by the educational sequence used in the schools of rhetoric. Early in the curriculum the students learned to praise illustrious men. One profits from this exercise, Quintilian (A.D. 35–A.D. 97) says, because "further wide knowledge of facts is thus acquired, from which examples may be drawn if circumstances so demand."[8] A funeral speech would be such a circumstance.

Whether a funeral speaker's focus was on the deceased or the ancestor's of the deceased, the audience was hearing praise, either of virtues or deeds. What, specifically, is an audience being asked to do, believe, or value in this instance? Is it sufficient to simply assert that the funeral speech has as its rhetorical goal, honoring the dead? More was involved than honor.

The lengthy passage from Dio Cassius quoted in chapter 5 indicates that the audience was being urged to emulate and exceed in quality the recounted deeds and accomplishments of the deceased. Most probably, this was the case. Still, the way in which the rhetoric of praise works, the rhetorical dynamic between a panegyrist's speech and the audience, remains unclear. Does one, for instance, simply hear a speech of praise and automatically seek to emulate or accord honor? With cause did Thucydides have Pericles in his funeral oration voice the cultural maxim, "for men can endure to hear others praised only so long as they can severally persuade themselves of their own ability to equal the actions recounted: when this point is passed, envy comes in and with it incredulity."[9] Laudation for a person does not automatically produce specific responses in an audience. Certain rhetorical principles need be employed if a speech of praise is to do more than simply be perceived as pleasing. The Roman rhetoricians clearly addressed these principles.

One cannot, according to Cicero and Quintilian, simply list admirable qualities—strength, wealth, etc.—since an individual did nothing to come by these qualities.[10] These are effects of nature or chance. What the deceased did with these personal endowments can be praised because it is in the realm of action, of choice-making, that an audience can glimpse the character and the virtues that make up the character of the dead person. If one used one's wealth, for example, to benefit the public, such an act would be perceived as deserving of praise and admiration.

Even in the territory of virtue certain character qualities are more praiseworthy than others: the personal quality of wisdom, for example, is a virtue but, when offered as a basis for praise may evoke pleasure but not admiration. Courageous action in the face of danger, however, as an item for praise can evoke admiration. The principles can be stated: the greater the altruism, the greater the honor; and the wider the public affected by the altruism, the greater the admiration. In Cicero's words:

> But the most welcome praise is that bestowed on deeds that appear to have been performed by brave men without

profit or reward; while those that also involve toil and personal danger supply very fertile topics for panegyric, because they admit of being narrated in a most eloquent style and of obtaining the readiest reception from the audience; for it is virtue that is profitable to others, and either toilsome or dangerous or at all events not profitable to its possessor, that is deemed to mark a man of outstanding merit.[11]

Cicero's pronouncement contains two clues—lack of reward and narrative form—to answer the question, "how does praise persuade?" An audience, attending to a funeral panegyric, must be made to hear a deficit, an unfair shortage of sorts, in the account of an unrewarded virtuous action. If a person is shown to have acted selflessly for the greater good of a collective, compensation is due. The collective, the beneficiary of the unrewarded and selfless act, is invited via the dynamic of laudation to repay, reward, or reciprocate in some way. This moral account is balanced when the audience, the affected collective, responds with admiration, esteem, heightened regard, and, possibly, a resolve to emulate. In the context of a funeral ritual, however, the deceased obviously cannot profit from the "repayment," but those in the audience can. How so?

The deceased's act of selfless valor creates a moral debt on the collective, an obligation that requires fulfillment. As is true in an economic system, debts must be repaid or the system ultimately collapses. In the moral sphere an act of heroism is typically given public recognition and, if the person is living, rewards, both real and symbolic, are given. In the case of a funeral, however, the hero is dead and a moral debt remains. The deceased cannot forgive the collective's liability; the collective cannot default because to do so jeopardizes the continuation of the collective itself. Moral bankruptcy destroys collectives. Those attending a funeral may do so to pay their respect, but, rhetorically, audiences hearing an account of altruistic, self-endangering actions done for the group must mentally raise their previous estimation of the deceased. The rhetorical dynamic results in an increased valuation and admiration of the deceased, thereby diminishing, but not fully compensating the indebtedness. Only keeping the deceased alive in memory offsets the obligation.

The members of the primary audience, in fact, receive moral instruction indirectly and by example, in the funeral speech. Insofar as each identifies with the action offered as praiseworthy the motive of altruism is also reinforced when one mentally says, "That is an admirable act and I could (should) behave the same way."

A second clue in Cicero's explanation of the rhetoric of praise is his quick reference to unrewarded acts of altruism "being narrated in a most eloquent style." The funeral speech is not an argument, but a story; not reasons with proofs, but it is a dramatic form capable of containing plot, character, and action.[12] Hearing a dramatic narrative, an audience is repositioned; that is, the message, in this case the panegyric, is not evaluated as are arguments or overt persuasive efforts. Narratives produce pleasure, not attitude sets of critical assessment of validity, refutation, or resistance. Narratives by their very nature invite participation, acceptance, and, if artfully done, some degree of identification. In a Roman funeral speech, then, as a part of the consolatory ritual, the narrative compliments the action and object languages whose rhetorical functions are designed to celebrate the life of the deceased and to reunite the community. It is not the deeds of the deceased that live on in the collective memory; instead, it is the virtues, the qualities of character reflected in the honored deeds of the deceased that live on.

Most regrettably, Latin literature contains no complete text of an actual funeral speech. Accounts of such orations can be read in the historians: Tiberius' speech for Tiberius in Dio Cassius and Antony's speech for Julius Caesar in Appian.[13] However, these accounts have far too many problems of authenticity, authorship, and accuracy to warrant offering them as representative illustrations. The private funeral oration of a husband in honor of his wife, preserved as an inscription, does offer a reader some understanding of the cultural practice. Since the names of both husband and wife are missing, scholars continue to argue about who, in fact, the principals were in the speech that has long been titled, "The Praise of Turia."[14] The text itself, most probably, represents the actual funeral speech given at the tomb rather than in the Forum, a practice sometimes performed, and ultimately carved in stone as an integral part of the burial monument.

As a funeral speech the oration represents what was customarily included in the first half of the standard panegyric, the praiseworthy qualities and deeds of the deceased. The traditional second section, laudation of the deceased's ancestors is either missing or was not made.

From the text we learn that the beloved wife was orphaned the day before her wedding by the murder of her parents. Turia, acting on her own and without help from her husband, pursued the case until the guilty were punished.

When Turia's father was killed, his will was protested and Turia's sister was to be cut out of the inheritance. The speaker says, "It was your firm decision that you would defend your father's written word; you would do this anyhow, you declared, by sharing your inheritance with your sister, if you were unable to uphold the validity of the will."[15] Turia won the case.

The speaker lists and acknowledges her domestic virtues but several of her demonstrably altruistic deeds are developed in dramatic detail. When the husband was exiled Turia used her own wealth and resources to ease his captivity; when robbers broke into their home, she "beat them back successfully."[16] The speaker next details yet another act of Turia's courage.

But I must say that the bitterest thing that happened to me in my life befell me through what happened to you. When thanks to the kindness and judgement of the absent Caesar Augustus I had been restored to my country as a citizen, Marcus Lepidus, his colleague, who was present, was confronted with your request concerning my recall, and you lay prostrate at his feet, and you were not only not raised up but were dragged away and carried off brutally like a slave. But although your body was full of bruises, your spirit was unbroken and you kept reminding him of Caesar's edict with its expression of pleasure at my reinstatement, and although you had to listen to insulting words and suffer cruel wounds, you pronounced the words of the edict in a loud voice, so that it should be known who was the cause of my deadly perils. This matter was soon to prove harmful for him.[17]

Turia's bravery in the face of brutality while saving her husband is next counterposed by a long account of personal sacrifice. When she learned she could not have children, Turia proposed a divorce, located a fertile wife for her husband, did not require a divorce payment, and offered to remain as a loyal mother-in-law. In the face of such devotion the speaker recalls his horror at the proposal and its prospect of separation.

In the concluding sections of the speech the speaker takes consolation "in the praise you have won," her fame, her glory, and her memory. He ends with the sentiment, "I pray that your *Di Manes* will grant you rest and protection."[18]

From this synopsis one can readily see, and possibly experience, the rhetorical dynamic of praise at work. As the narrator, the speaker has a relationship to the deceased that renders the accuracy of the accounts unquestionably incredible. In the context of bereavement one does not expect, nor would one tolerate, negative or disparaging words spoken of the dead, consequently, any balanced recounting is culturally prohibited. Implicit within the narrated episodes is an evaluative comparison, a form of opposition capable of resonating with the arrayed sets of symbols in the ritual, which set off any number of moral contrasts. For example, other wives are afforded a model of moral behavior; other married couples, as audience to the text, are instructed in the rubric of compassionate devotion; other community members, as audience, are rhetorically invited to offer admiration, honor, and emulation; and those experiencing grief and bereavement are summoned both to empathize with the speaker's loss and to join with the speaker in continuing life.

Literary Forms of Consolation

Near the beginning of his review of the literary consolation genre, Hans Betz identifies both the probable origin of the practice and one of the problems involved in interpreting them.

It is likely enough that written consolations began when letter writing became the means of communication between individuals who could not meet face-to-face, and if that is so they came to exist in an area where the distinction between literature and life is particularly hard to draw. The letter form quickly became a literary convention itself, with the result that we cannot always be sure whether a given consolation, once written, was immediately handed to a messenger for delivery to the addressee or to a copyist for reproduction and circulation among the writer's literary audience.[19]

As travel became more commonplace individuals would be more likely to be absent when a death occurred. Similarly, as writing itself became more commonplace, written words of consolation could, and did, serve as surrogates for traditional, oral forms. Therefore, one can read consolatory literature in the same way one might read a consolatory speech. Still, given the fact that a consolation is placed in writing and published one must recognize that literary criteria may be more appropriate than rhetorical standards in interpreting them.[20] Classical authors, one must remember, were schooled in rhetoric and their training in the art of persuasion did influence their written composition, regardless of genre.

Letters, essays, and poems addressed to a bereaved individual were crafted by both Greeks and Romans.[21] Crantor's (ca. 300 B.C.) letter to Hippocles whose children had died, although no longer extant, served as a respected model for many writers. Epicurus (342 B.C.–268 B.C.), Dio Chrysostum (A.D. 40–A.D. 95), and Plutarch (A.D. 50–A.D. 120) also published consolations. Also extant in Latin are letters authored by Sulpicius, Cicero, Pliny, and Seneca. Two distinct sets of influence can be seen in these later consolatory works: the philosophical and the rhetorical.

Each of the several schools of philosophy, active in the Hellenistic and Roman Eras, taught differing views on the nature of death. For the Stoics death was natural and therefore not an evil and not a cause for sorrow. Epicureans held that death merely involved the dissolution of body and soul and, accordingly, was not a condition to fear. By recalling prior pleasures with the deceased, the Epicureans claimed, the pain of loss is reduced. Peripatetics, on the other hand, believed that emotions ought to be expressed, but only in moderation. In almost any given example of literary consolation one can find distinct imprints from each philosophical school. Most Romans were eclectic and refused to adhere strictly or solely to any single set of philosophical tenets.

If one can accept Cicero as representing and reflecting the contributions from the schools of rhetoric to the task of alleviating grief, the role of verbal persuasion is more than evident. Cicero believed that an orator needed to combine philosophy and rhetoric, wisdom and eloquence, thus, for him, any attempt at consolation would draw upon both disciplines.[22] In his *de Oratore*, for example, Cicero delineates the several types of rhetorical problems (*quaestiones*) with which a speaker must become adept. In the division of treating moral conduct he says: "Those referring to conduct either deal with the discussion of duty—the department that asks what action is right and proper, a topic comprising the whole subject of the virtues and vices—or are employed either in producing or in allaying or removing some emotion. This class comprises modes of exhortation, reproach, consolation, compassion and every method of exciting, and also, if so indicated by the situation, of allaying all the emotions."[23] Intense personal grief at the loss of a loved one would be an emotional state requiring language designed to ease, lighten, and mitigate. While philosophy could provide reasoned analyses about grief, rhetoric provided a method for making such analyses operate in practical instances.

When his own daughter died Cicero composed the *Tusculan Disputations*, a treatise in which he sought to console himself. In addition to reviewing what philosophers have said on the subject of consolation, Cicero also and at length displays the resources rhetoric holds. One must argue, he says, that death is not an evil.[24] Then, depending on the circumstances and recency of a death he recommends various arrangements of the arguments.[25]

A number of Greek rhetorical theorists in subsequent centuries included prescriptions for consolation in their treatises: Theon (first century A.D.), pseudo-Dionysius (second century A.D.), and Menander (third century A.D.). Each offers advice about the inclusion or exclusion of lamentations, each offers topics to use, and each defines structural arrangements to follow in constructing a consolation. Outlines of these treatises have already been presented in chapter 4.

To illustrate the ways in which philosophy served rhetoric in the cause of literary consolation, an abbreviated critique of Cicero's letter to Titius will suffice.[26]

In 46 B.C. an otherwise unknown Roman, Titius, suffered the death of his children. Nothing is known about the wife, the family, or the circumstances of the deaths. Cicero addresses a letter of consolation to Titius, the father.

After indicating that he, too, is grieving and, therefore, knows the pain of sorrow, Cicero announces that he will "offer you some such measure of consolation as might mitigate, if it could not succeed in remedying, your sorrow" (Section 1). A disingenuous beginning, this. In the ensuing sections of the letter, Cicero clearly intends to remedy not simply mitigate. Yet, by offering his reader a lesser but by no means unattractive goal and should his rhetorical effort fail, as it surely must in a situation of intense bereavement, readers other than Titius could credit his argument as probably successful. For readers other than Titius, too, the act of consoling another offers evidence attesting to Cicero's ethical good will, his compassion and benevolence.

Immediately, Cicero injects a section developed around the Stoic observation that it is in the nature of things that humans should suffer misfortune and one must accept them. Recognizing that, although the observation is true, the tenet does not offer much consolation, Cicero begins to reconfigure the death. Given the wretched state of affairs in Rome, he suggests, by comparison, one who has lost children ought not to be pitied. He implies that, had they lived, they would grow up in a destructing world of political and social ugliness. Digressing from the theme of "be grateful they did not live to endure a world in tumult," Cicero adds a pair of disjunctions:

You grieve:
either because you are thinking about how the
loss affects you (implying selfishness)
or because you are thinking about the fate of
your dead children (implying selflessness)
But, "There is no evil in death" because
either the dead still have sensation and are
not really dead

or the dead have no sensation and, therefore,
cannot experience misery. (Section 4)

Unless one were to mount a refutation based on the material
and formal validity of the premises or advance a rejoinder
based on the probabilities of the opposite being a more believ-
able case—efforts preempted in the context of offering consolation—Cicero's paired disjunctions, a type of rhetorical
sorites, do afford a reasonable position from which to consider
the deaths and the basis for one's grief.

Cicero returns to his theme that the present state of the
world is such that a death is a blessing in disguise and con-
cludes the section by saying, "It follows then if you can rid yourself of this one idea that any evil, as you suppose, can have
befallen those you loved, it means a very material abatement
of your grief" (Section 5). Incrementalism and apparent com-
pleteness underscore this passage. Titius is told, in effect, that
absolutely no reasons exist for thinking about the fate of his
children. Assuming one of the two possible causes of grief to-
tally dismissed, he proceeds to address the second, Titius' sense
of personal loss.

Cicero launches a salvo of moral commonplaces at Titius:
you, yourself, can control your sorrow; you have always overcome difficulties before, do so now; even women end their
mourning eventually but a wise man knows that death is inevitable and, knowing this you can end your grief now (Section
6).

Cicero ends by portraying himself as "a very sincere well-
wisher and friend" (Section 6).

As literature, the letter is unified, coherent, forceful, and
forthright. Cicero's epistolary effort permits a reader to over-
hear a wise and concerned human being offering aid to the op-
pressed, an act of secular charity.

As rhetoric, the arguments can be traced back across the
centuries to the Sophists of fifth century Athens (see chapter
4). Death is a fact of nature (*physis*) but the perceptions of
death (*nomos*) can be analyzed (philosophy), addressed, and ar-
gued (rhetoric). Not until the emergence of literary consolation
does rhetorical argument appear centuries after the Greek
Sophists. Why this was so remains an interesting question.

NOTES

1. Fridericus Vollmer, "Laudationum Funebrium Romanorum Historia et Reliquarum Editio," *Neue Jahrbucher fur Philologie* (Suppl. 18, 1891), 445–528; Enrica Malcovati, *Oratorum Romanorum Fragmenta* (Milan, 1955), 468–76; O. C. Crawford, "Laudatio Funebris," *Classical Journal* 27 (1941):17–21; M. Durry, "Laudatio funebris et rhetorique," *Revue de Philologie* 16 (1942):105–114; George Kennedy, "Antony's Speech at Caesar's Funeral," *The Quarterly Journal of Speech* 54 (1968):99–106; Hubert Martin, Jr. and Jane E. Phillips, "Consolatio Ad Uxorem (Moralia 608A–612B)," in *Plutarch's Ethical Writings and Early Christian Literature*, ed. Hans Dieter Betz, 394–413 (Leiden: E. J. Brill, 1978); Erik Wistrand, *The So-Called Laudatio Turiae: Introduction, Text, Translation, Commentary* (Berlingska Boktryckeriet, Lund: Acta Universitatis Gothoburgensis, 1976); Wilhelm Kierdorf, *Laudatio Funebris: Interpretationem und Untersuchungen zur Entwicklung der Romischen Leichenrede* (Meisenheim am Glan: Verlag Anton Hain, 1980).
2. Plutarch, *The Lives of the Noble Grecians and Romans*, trans. John Dryden (New York: The Modern Library, 1952), 122.
3. *The Roman Antiquities of Dionysius of Halicarnassus*, trans. Earnest Cary (Cambridge: Harvard University Press, 1937), 17:4–6.
4. Cf. *Corpus Inscriptionum Latinarum*, 14, no's. 3579, 10230, 1527. Also Crawford, "Laudatio," 21–22.
5. Polybius, 6.53.1.
6. Cicero, *de Oratore*, trans. E. W. Sutton and H. Rackam (Cambridge, MA: Harvard University Press, 1959), 2.10.44–45. For the same sentiment, 2.74.341:

> For the Greeks themselves have constantly thrown off masses of panegyrics, designed more for reading and entertainment, or for giving a laudatory account of some person, than for the practical purposes of public life with which we are now concerned: there are Greek books containing panegyrics of Themistocles, Aristides, Agesilaus, Epaminondas, Philip, Alexander and others; whereas our Roman commendatory speeches that we make in the forum have either the bare and unadorned brevity of evidence to a person's character or are written to be delivered as a funeral speech, which is by no means a suitable occasion for parading one's distinction in rhetoric.

7. Cicero, *de Oratore*, 2.10.46.

8. *The Institutio Oratoria of Quintilian*, trans. H. E. Butler (New York: G. P. Putnam's Sons, 1933), 2.4.20.
9. *The Complete Writings of Thucydides: The Peloponnesian War*, trans. R. Crawley (New York: The Modern Library), 103.
10. Cicero, *de Oratore*, 2.84.342ff.; Quintilian, 3.7.15.
11. Cicero, *de Oratore*, 2.85.346.
12. Cf. W. R. Fisher, "Rationality and the Logic of Good Reasons," *Philosophy and Rhetoric* 13 (1980):121–130; ———, "Narration as a Human Communication Paradigm: The Case of Public Moral Argument," *Communication Monographs* 51 (1984):1–22; ———, *Human Communications as Narration: Toward a Philosophy of Reason, Value, and Action* (Columbia, SC: University of South Carolina Press, 1987); ———, "Clarifying the Narrative Paradigm," *Communication Monographs* 56 (1989):55–58.
13. Cf. Vollmer, "Laudationum," 480ff.
14. Wistrand, *So-Called*, 9.
15. Wistrand, *So-Called*, 21.
16. Wistrand, *So-Called*, 25.
17. Wistrand, *So-Called*, 25.
18. Wistrand, *So-Called*, 31. *Di Manes* is usually translated as "the gods of the dead."
19. Betz, *Plutarch's Ethical*, 406.
20. Cf. George Kennedy, *Classical Rhetoric and Its Christian and Secular Tradition from Ancient to Modern Times* (Chapel Hill: University of North Carolina Press, 1980), ch. 6. Also Richard Leo Enos, *The Literate Mode of Cicero's Legal Rhetoric* (Carbondale: Southern Illinois University Press, 1988).
21. Collections of references, sources, and analyses of consolatory discourse are available in C. Buresch, "Consolationum a Graecis Romanisque scriptarum historia critica," *Leipziger Studien zur Classischen Philologie* 9 (1886):3–170. Also R. Kassel, "Untersuchungen zur griechischen und romischen Konsolations-literatur," *Zetemata* 18 (Munich, 1958). Less complete, but generally more accessible, is Martin R. P. McGuire, "The Early Christian Funeral Oration," in *The Fathers of the Church*, ed. Roy Joseph Deferrari, vol. 22, vii–xxi (New York: Fathers of the Church, Inc., 1953).
22. Cicero, *de Oratore*, 3.30.123.
23. Cicero, *de Oratore*, 3.30.118.
24. Cicero, *Tusculan Disputations*, trans. John Edward King (Cambridge: Harvard University Press, 1958), 1.112–17.
25. Cicero, *Tusculan Disputations*, 3.76–77.
26. Cicero, *The Letters to his Friends*, trans. W. Glynn Williams (Cambridge, MA: Harvard University Press, 1979), 5.16.

Postscript

This study began with the premise that, in a funeral ritual, sets of symbols are placed in opposition to function rhetorically on the participants. After viewing the evidence from the Classical Era and studying the arguments drawn from the evidence each reader, necessarily, will judge whether the evidence is sufficient and the degree to which the premise is established. In these final pages, however, some observations about rhetoric's relationship to community, ritual, and consolation need to be made. To these I turn.

Rhetoric and Community

A contemporary reader, no doubt, using one's own experiences of death, funeral rituals, and consolation as vantage positions for interpretation, will compare the Greco-Roman practices to those in his or her present-day communities. Differences exist, to be sure. Nonetheless, the interplay between community and rituals of consolation remain in sharp focus within such a comparison. What, precisely, constitutes a community may never be adequately resolved but certain traits, behaviors, and characteristics seem to be important parts of any such definition. Humans who share locale, language, history, and customs and who are interdependent for the continuation of the group and who also share a set of values can be said to be a community. Persuasion, by its very nature, relies on the preexistence of communal values—values internalized, known, and practiced by the members of a community. If they are to resolve differences, adopt plans, celebrate accomplishments, and cope with threats to the group, communities must rely on rhetoric in its various forms and formats, its verbal and other-than-verbal registers.

When death threatens a community, a powerful form of rhetoric is needed to eliminate the threat. In this study the form of opposition predominates and controls the rhetorical enterprises designed to elicit consolation. Might opposition be the strongest of the rhetorical forms? Perhaps. The question deserves a more extended discussion than is possible here. Certainly, the role of opposition in the Greco-Roman funeral rituals is evidence of its power.

When death threatens a community, a powerful—and unusual—format of rhetoric is used. This format is more akin to a dramatistic modality than to the typical speaker-message-audience model. Death calls for a communal rhetoric in which the community both produces and consumes the consolatory, persuasive messages. In Burke's terms, acts, actions, and actors merge. The community persuades and is persuaded. Communities are sustained by rituals and, as this study indicates, rhetoric plays a significant role in ritual. Since this is so, the importance of rhetoric to a community and to the maintenance of the community is greater than usually believed. Rhetoric, the rationale of instrumental and symbolic behavior, lies at the very heart of community.

Rhetoric in Ritual

Rhetoric, as a discipline, has at its core the study of human communication. By definition rhetoric necessarily involves itself with the energized means of communicating, with the purposes of the act, and with the audiences addressed. Audiences, in a broad sense, are collectives with common interests, communities with shared objectives. When a community, as a community, engages in ritual activity, meaningful symbols are used. Analyzing what these meanings are, how they function, and on whom they function is the province of rhetoric. Ritual can be and need be analyzed from a rhetorical perspective. Why so?

Those who study ritual as ritual—the sociologists and anthropologists cited in the early chapters of this study—agree that rituals are powerful; rituals preserve social order; and rituals directly influence and affect how participants acquire, develop, and alter their central beliefs about the universe. Indeed, one can safely claim that a group's rituals define and determine who they are, their identity, and their central values. A social nexus with such far-reaching effect deserves to be studied, rhetorically, to learn how communities communicate and what purposes communication serves in ritual. An increased understanding of ritual as a communicative set of human actions results from applying the methods of rhetoric to ritual.

All cultures, much like humans, seek to preserve themselves and, in ritual, the culture engages in symbolic activity to this end. Change in any of its various forms is an assault, with varying degrees of potential harm, on the self-preservation of the collective. Births, marriages, and deaths each pose the need to respond to significant changes in roles, status, and membership. Again, viewing ritual from a rhetorical perspective permits one to learn how communication through symbols is used to both adapt to and resist changes that threaten the continuation of the audience—the collective itself.

What, then, is persuasive in ritual? Since only consolatory rituals in the Classical Era were analyzed in this study, the answer must be restricted to that type of ritual. If nothing else, the evidence in the preceding chapters ought to clearly indicate that in these cases symbols are not used haphazardly. On the contrary, sets of symbols are repeatedly selected, placed, and arranged in meaningful forms, and timed to appear at various stages of the ceremonies. As a series of rhetorical acts the funeral ritual appears carefully orchestrated to persuade the participants to separate from the deceased, to marginalize the deceased in the midst of the living, and to reunite the living. Learning what factors are capable of persuading in these circumstances and for these objectives is a valuable enterprise best undertaken from the vantage point of rhetoric.

Traditionally, rhetorical analysis is usually developed to study discursive language—verbal symbols used in communication. As this study revealed, however, the discursive language of eulogy was noticeably absent in many of the funeral rituals and, moreover, when present, were small parts of the ceremony and most often served political functions. The received tradition of rhetorical theory and critical methodology is of less assistance in dealing with a form of ritual that relies mostly on action and object languages. That such is the case should be a cause for excitement and a sense of opportunity. Those who work with contemporary theories of persuasion might profitably begin developing better methods for analyzing nondiscursive symbols used in the practice of persuasion. True, Burke, Kertzner, Turner, and others have started explorations in this direction, but, to use a cliche, much uncharted territory remains. This study of consolatory rhetoric and its dependence on nondiscursive symbols suggests an analogical approach for reading these symbols.

Stated more precisely, perhaps, than is evident in the chapters, one can begin with the observation that symbols—discursive and nondiscursive—are present, presented, and experienced. No symbol has meaning until it is placed with another in some sort of relationship. Few would disagree with these general characterizations, but important differences between these two categories of symbols exist. Nondiscursive symbols, the action and object languages specified in this study, derive their persuasive power from their condensation of meaning, multivocality, and richness of ambiguity. Most uses of discursive language do not possess these qualities. One can proceed, however, analogically. In our discursive language practice, for example, our verbs are typically in the indicative mood expressing, as Webster says, "an act, state or occurrence as actual, or to ask a question of fact." As readers and listeners of discursive language we are focused, fixed, narrowed, limited, and restricted. Our verbs can be active or passive and admit to tense or temporality; our words can be structured in any number of rhetorical forms.

One can begin the study and analysis of nondiscursive symbols, analogically, by interpreting them at a grammatical level as possessing the traits of the subjunctive mood. As such, action and object languages may be seen as possessing supposition, desire, hypothesis, or possibility. Nondiscursive symbols— the marring of one's face, decorating the corpse, military maneuvers, etc.—in the preceding chapters are always in the active voice and present tense. For participants in the funeral ritual, nondiscursive symbols exist in the present and participants are not fixed, limited, or restricted as with discursive language. In this study, the rhetorical form of opposition predominates and best explains how the persuasive effort of collective consolation is achieved. The other-than-verbal languages, however, do seem to operate as does verbal language in the subjunctive mood.

Rhetoric for Consolation

Death invariably causes grief which, if not addressed, can debilitate, damage, and possibly destroy a social group. The threat to a group's self-preservation is real. For the group or the community to continue functioning, significant changes must take place. The dead person must be redefined and transformed into a different kind of existence; the living must be persuaded to choose life and the living community rather than succumb to the powerfully detrimental emotions of loss, anguish, and sorrow. The rituals studied in the preceding chapters offer ample evidence to claim that discursive language does not have the resources to redefine, transform, and persuade in this particular rhetorical situation. Not only is it the case that "words cannot express one's sorrow," but, quite probably, words alone cannot meet the demands of consoling a social group. Communicative symbols in different and more efficacious registers, the registers of action and object languages, are needed. Two questions arise. Why is it not possible to persuade, with verbal language, a social group into a state of consolation? Why do action and object languages succeed?

The answers reside in consolatory ritual itself. The ones investigated in this study all extend across a period of time; no single orator could conceivably present a reasoned case for three to seven days. Moreover, an address, even if it were somehow possible, requires a passive audience of listeners rather than an active audience of participants who are also producing the ritual. Then too, an hypothetical speech of consolation in the sense used here cannot simultaneously focus on both the dead person and the living community. No verbal language has this capacity—action and object languages do.

To borrow Aristotle's term, the final cause of persuasion is not a speaker or a message but the individual himself or herself. Ultimately, we reach a state of conviction about something by ourselves. In the consolatory rituals presented in this study, the action and object languages work by indirection. That is, they suggest, allude, and insinuate. Their characteristic ambiguity invites attention, participation, and interpretation. Discourse directs; nondiscursive languages request. Discourse exhorts; nondiscursive languages entice. Participants in a consolatory ritual, I believe, are more likely to accept redefinition, transformation, mortality, and the continuation of their social group through the indirect rhetoric offered by nondiscursive symbols. Such was certainly the case for the Greeks and Romans.

Select Bibliography

Adams, John Quincey. *Lectures on Rhetoric and Oratory*. Ed. J. Jeffrey Auer and Jerald L. Banninga. New York: Russell and Russell, 1962.

Alexiou, Margaret. *The Ritual Lament in Greek Tradition*. London: Cambridge University Press, 1974.

Bailey, Dudley. *Essays on Rhetoric*. New York: Oxford University Press, 1965.

Bennett, Larry J. and Wm. Blake Tyrrell. "Sophocles' *Antigone* and Funeral Oratory." In *American Journal of Philology* 111 (1990):441–56.

Bitzer, Lloyd F. "The Rhetorical Situation." In *Philosophy and Rhetoric* 1 (1968):1–14.

Burgess, Theodore C. *Epideictic Literature*. Chicago: University of Chicago Press, 1902.

Booth, Wayne C. "The Scope of Rhetoric Today: A Polemical Excursion." In *The Prospect of Rhetoric: Report of the National Development Project*. Eds. Lloyd F. Bitzer and Edwin Black. Engelwood Cliffs, NJ: Prentice-Hall, Inc., 1971.

Bowers, John Waite and Donovan J. Ochs. *The Rhetoric of Agitation and Control*. Reading, MA: Addison-Wesley Publishing Co., Inc., 1971.

Bryant, Donald C. "Rhetoric: Its Function and Scope." In *The Quarterly Journal of Speech* 39 (December 1953):401–24.

Burke, Kenneth. *Language as Symbolic Action: Essays on Life, Literature, and Method*. Berkeley, CA: University of California Press, 1966.

———. *A Rhetoric of Motives*. New York: The World Publishing Company, 1962.

Campbell, Paul Newell. *Rhetoric—Ritual: A Study of the Communicative and Aesthetic Dimensions of Language*. Belmont, CA: Dickenson Publishing Co., 1972.

Cannadine, David and Simon Price, eds. *Rituals of Royalty: Power and Ceremonial in Traditional Societies*. New York: Cambridge University Press, 1987.

Carter, Michael F. "The Ritual Functions of Epideictic Rhetoric: The Case of Socrates' Funeral Oration." *Rhetorica* 3 (1991):209–32.

Cary, M. J. and T. J. Haarhoff. *Life and Thought in the Greek and Roman World*. London: Methuen and Co. Ltd., reprint 1968.

Curl, James Stevens. *A Celebration of Death: An Introduction to Some of the Buildings, Monuments, and Settings of Funerary Architecture in the Western European Tradition*. New York: Charles Scribner's Sons, 1980.

Durkheim, Emile. *The Elementary Forms of the Religious Life*. Trans. J. W. Swain. New York: The Free Press, 1965.

Fisher, Walter R. *Rhetoric: A Tradition in Transition: Studies in Honor of Donald C. Bryant*. East Lansing, MI: Michigan State University Press, 1974.

Geertz, Clifford. "Religion as a Cultural System." In *Anthropological Approaches to the Study of Religion*. Ed. Michael Banton. London: Tavistock, 1966.

Kearl, Michael C. *Endings: A Sociology of Death and Dying*. New York: Oxford University Press, 1989.

Kennedy, George. "Antony's Speech at Caesar's Funeral." *The Quarterly Journal of Speech* 54 (1968):99–106.

———. *Aristotle on Rhetoric: A Theory of Civic Discourse*. New York: Oxford University Press, 1991.

Kertzer, David I. *Ritual, Politics, and Power*. New Haven: Yale University Press, 1988.

Kurtz, Donna C. and John Boardman. *Greek Burial Customs*. Ithaca, NY: Cornell University Press, 1971.

La Fontaine, J. S., ed. *The Interpretation of Ritual: Essays in Honour of A. I. Richards*. London: Tavistock, 1972.

Leach, Edmund. *Culture and Communication: The Logic by Which Symbols are Connected: An Introduction to the Use of Structuralist Analysis in Social Anthropology*. New York: Cambridge University Press, 1976.

Lloyd, Geoffrey E. R. *Polarity and Analogy: Two Types of Argumentation in Greek Thought*. Cambridge: Cambridge University Press, 1966.

MacAloon, John J., ed. *Rite, Drama, Festival, Spectacle: Rehearsals Toward a Theory of Cultural Performance*. Philadelphia: The Institute for the Study of Human Science, 1984.

Mackin, James A., Jr. "Schismogenesis and Community: Pericles' Funeral Oration." In *The Quarterly Journal of Speech* 77 (August 1991):251–62.

McKeon, Richard Peter. *Rhetoric: Essays in Invention and Discovery*. Woodbridge, CT: Ox Bow Press, 1987.

Morris, Ian. *Burial and Ancient Society: The Rise of the Greek City State*. New York: Cambridge University Press, 1987.

Nichols, Marie Hochmuth. *Rhetoric and Criticism*. Baton Rouge: Louisiana State University Press, 1963.

Nicolet, Claude. *The World of the Citizen in Republican Rome*. Trans. P. S. Falla. Berkeley: University of California Press, 1988.

Perelman, Chaim and L. Olbrechts-Tyteca Perelman. *The New Rhetoric: A Treatise on Argumentation*. Trans. John Wilkinson and Purcell Weaver. Notre Dame, IN: University of Notre Dame Press, 1969.

Powell, Anton. *Athens and Sparta: Constructing Greek Political and Social History from 478 B.C.* Portland, OR: Areopagitica Press, 1988.

Poulakos, Takis. "Historiographies of the Tradition of Rhetoric: A Brief History of Classical Funeral Orations." In *Western Journal of Speech Communication* 54 (Spring 1990):172–88.

———. "The Historical Intervention of Gorgias' *Epitaphios*: The Genre of Funeral Oration and the Athenian Institution of Public Burials." *Pretext* 1–2 (1989):90–99.

Price, S. R. F. *Rituals and Power: The Roman Imperial Cult in Asia Minor*. New York: Cambridge University Press, 1984.

Rankin, H. D. *Sophists, Socratics, and Cynics*. Totowa, NJ: Barnes and Noble Books, 1983.

Scott, John A. *Homer and His Influence*. New York: Cooper Square Publishers, Inc., 1963.

Sealey, Raphael. *A History of the Greek City States, 700–338 B.C.* Berkeley, CA: University of California Press, 1976.

Shaughnessy, James D., ed. *The Roots of Ritual*. Grand Rapids, MI: William B. Eerdmans Publishing Company, 1973.

Thonssen, Lester. *Selected Readings in Rhetoric and Public Speaking*. New York: The H. W. Wilson Co., 1942.

Thonssen, Lester and A. Craig Baird. *Speech Criticism*. New York: The Ronald Press Co., 1948.

Vickers, Brian. *In Defense of Rhetoric*. New York: Oxford University Press, 1988.

Warner, W. Lloyd. *The Living and the Dead*. New Haven: Yale University Press, 1959.

Ziolkowski, John E. *Thucydides and the Tradition of Funeral Speeches at Athens*. Salem, NH: The Ayer Co., 1981.

Index

Achilleus, 38
action language, 4, 64, 89, 121–22
aggregation, 45, 53ff.
altruism, 107
ambiguity, 7, 121
Anaximenses, 105
antitheses, 75
Antonius, 105, 109
appropriateness, 22
Aristotle, 62, 77
Athenian State, 61ff.
Augustus, 97

Baccylides, 69
bereavement, 16
Brutus, 104
burial, 53

cemetary, 33
Cicero, 105–6, 108, 112–13, 114ff.
Cleisthenes, 61
community, 23, 31–32, 44, 52, 118
consolation, 21ff., 61, 86
consolatory literature, 104, 112
constancy, 87
Crantor, 112
cremation, 40, 93
custom, 62
cypress, 65

death, 21ff.
Demosthenes, 77

denial, 25
Dio Cassius, 107, 109
Dio Chrysostum, 112
Dionysius of Halicarnassus, 105
disjunctions, 115
Draco, 61

effigy, 100
Epicureans, 112
Epicurus, 112
epideictic, 31
Etruscans, 84–85
eulogy, 31
exigence, 20

fasting, 39
feasting, 40, 56ff.
Forum, 93, 97
funeral games, 40
funeral oration, 66, 67ff., 95
funeral ritual, 1ff., 6, 28ff., 30, 32, 94, 118
funus translaticum, 88

gens, 86
Germanicus, 97
Gorgias, 77
grave goods, 40, 42, 54
gravity, 87
grief, 24ff., 38, 122

Hippocles, 112
Homer, 37ff.
Hyperides, 77